THE
BLACK
SUITCASE

JOHN E.
MORRISON

 FriesenPress

Suite 300 - 990 Fort St
Victoria, BC, V8V 3K2
Canada

www.friesenpress.com

Copyright © 2020 by John E. Morrison
First Edition — 2020

Foreword by Thomas Wall and Universary of Limerick.

Thanks to the National Geographic Magazie and the Limerick Christmas Gazette 1941 for the photo of the Creagh Lane school milk and bun break. I would like to dedicate this book to all the boys.

ISBN
978-1-5255-7699-7 (Hardcover)
978-1-5255-7700-0 (Paperback)
978-1-5255-7701-7 (eBook)

1. BIOGRAPHY & AUTOBIOGRAPHY, PERSONAL MEMOIRS

Distributed to the trade by The Ingram Book Company

ACKNOWLEDGEMENTS

I would like to take this opportunity to thank Tom Wall, the last inmate of Glin, for your efforts in bringing the damning evidence against the industrial school to the proper authorities. Without your bravery many more would have suffered. To the University of Limerick, I would like to extend my gratitude for not only aiding in bringing light to the atrocities taking place in Glin Industrial School, but also for allowing me to source the material necessary to create this memoir, I am in your debt. A heartfelt thank you to my family for your continued assistance in my writing endeavour. Be it with proofreading, photography or just emotional support you are all loved beyond measure. Lastly to Julianne McCallum, the Publishing Specialist, and her hardworking team at Friesen Press for allowing me to share my voice and experiences with the world. This has been a labour of love and to see it come to fruition has been a dream come true.

"My scars remind me that I did indeed survive my deepest wounds. That in itself is an accomplishment. And they bring to mind something else, too. They remind me that the damage life has inflicted on me has, in many places, left me stronger and more resilient. What hurt me in the past has actually made me better equipped to face the present."
-Steve Goodier

THE BLACK SUITCASE

A MEMOIR

The black suitcase holds all of my memories of my childhood in Limerick City, Ireland and beyond. It informs me that I was born to a loving mother in the Island Field better known as St. Mary's Park, on August 29, 1935, ten days after the estate was completed—the first male child born. This suitcase, filled with photographs and letters, has been in my possession since my mother gave it to me before she fled to England in 1949.

When I look back over the eighty-four years that my memory affords me, I smile and I cry. I cry at my teen years to the age of sixteen, and I smile because of the hand on my shoulder. I do not know whose hand, but it would guide me in the right direction. I took my bearings for life from Limerick and the Island Field.

I may make a few mistakes in this story of memories, but it is the real and true account of a very fortunate boy. Some names and places have been changed and pseudonyms are used in the "investigation into child abuse" at St. Joseph's Industrial School in the beautiful town of Glin.

My boyhood in Limerick was not miserable. On the contrary, it was a happy childhood up to age thirteen and six months, the memories of which I am forever thankful for, except for the terrible beating at Creagh Lane Gerald Griffin School.

I am a survivor of child abuse and this is my story.

1949

The number of children held in St. Joseph's Industrial School in the village of Glin, County Limerick, Ireland peaked to 212 in 1949 from 211 in the year 1948 and from there on decreased yearly. I was sentenced on February 5, 1949 at age thirteen, six months, and 160 days old to be released at age sixteen.

My father was in England and my mother had left Ireland for England with Joe, her boyfriend, after my twelve-year-old sister died May 31, 1949 at her grandmother's house where the courts had sent my brother and sisters, citing neglect by our mother. Our mother was close to being destitute, and we had lived as squatters in an old, abandoned butcher's shop; Number 10 Robert's Street with no heat but a fireplace and a straw-filled bag for a mattress on the concrete floor. A blanket covered the large window, and we had no toilet or bathroom but a bucket, which was emptied in a drain on the dark street. From that point on fatherless, at approximately twelve years of age, I took on the role as the eldest, to provide for the family. This I did by missing school too many times, to beg for food door to door (called mooching), mostly at the wealthy homes on Ennis Road where actor Richard Harris's family lived, I learned later in life. After knocking on the doors, my lament was, "Have you a piece of bread or a penny please?" I also worked at the market on Saturdays. I may have been sentenced for several reasons, which only Judge Gleeson, "The Hanging Judge," as we called him, would know; "stealing" Father Lee's old bike, mooching, parent unable to control child, poverty, and/or destitution. Forty-eight percent of the children committed to Glin were there as a direct consequence of their impoverished backgrounds. This is one report by a Doctor McCabe to the superior at the school.

1. Porridge should be served at breakfast. Each boy should be allowed at least a quarter of a pound of meat at each meal at which meat is served.
2. The clothes should be improved.
3. The sanitary annexe should be kept in better order.
4. Rubber aprons and Wellington boots should be provided for the boys in the laundry.
5. There is the need for the provision of a new bathing annexe.
6. The dampness in the walls of the dormitories should be attended to. It is understood that you will arrange to have this matter attended to in the summer of 1947.

To number one: We served ourselves through our table monitor, (one of the boys) with tasteless porridge, no sugar, and a tin mug of creamy milk right out of the cows on our farm. At home I relied on a bun and bottle of milk supplied by the school, which was more enjoyable.

Number two: At home I had my short pants and a wool ganzey (pullover) with snotty sleeves.

Number three: Was better than the bucket at home.

Number four: At home I had no boots at all and a bucket (the same one as above) for laundry and a scrubbing board.

Number five: At home we had a zinc tin bath in front of the fire, which was a luxury.

Number six: The walls at the school were still damp in 1949, '50, and '51. Nothing had changed.

This introduction to my memories gives a clear account of St. Joseph's Industrial School, (Glin), Co. Limerick; circa, 1872-1966.

Some of the words I'll be using are the way we spoke in Limerick City. "Hush" and "Whisht" mean be quiet. "Meself" means myself. "Nosh" means not. "Jasus" means Jesus. "Gom" means fool. "Wellingtons" means rubber boots. "Ginnet," means the offspring of a horse and donkey. "Mooched" means missed school. "Gods" means upstairs. "Me" means my. "Idgit" means fool, same as gom. "Rack" means comb.

John E. Morrison.

MEMORIES ARE MADE OF THIS

The ship rolled gently; the bow one minute pointing at the blushing moon and then sending shudders along her ageing deck as she violently crashed back on to the Irish Sea, sending refreshing droplets of salt water on to my face, hiding the tears. In Dun Laoghaire in the Port of Dublin, distant lights now were seen as we sailed toward the port of Holyhead, which to me was in a foreign land called Wales.

I was sixteen and three months of age and in the company of a man whom I addressed as "Sir," my father. I watched him lying on the broad rail, his arms folded across his chest, eyes closed. I stared at this man and tried to remember my childhood; his part in my life in St. Mary's Park, better known as Island Field—a task that was not too easy. *It would have been around 1942 or 43,* I thought. It may as well have been 1842 or 1843, for conditions had not changed in Limerick City except for the first new corporation houses on King's Island, Island Field. I remembered sitting on the doorstep of the house, keeping a tight hold on the greyhound, Tuppence, and listening to my father inside. He was smashing onto the concrete floor the table and the four chairs and the china cabinet and crockery, which were the pride and joy of our mother. He had been drinking and was in a rage, for which I would much later learn the cause. My three younger sisters and brother were hiding upstairs on the bed as I cried with my mother, who I could hear inside.

That cold November night on the ship I was thankful for the salty spray on my face. *He will never see me shed a tear again,* I thought, not since that eventful day that he had stepped over my cowering body on the doorstep, leaving behind a heart-broken mother and bewildered children.

"Shawnee!" The call could be heard across the Shannon to the distillery, and as far as the Treaty Stone in Thomond Gate. Our mother had the voice of a soprano, and everyone in the Island Field knew it. I was five years old and had long since started wandering from the confines of the little front garden where the pink tea-rose bush grew. Breeda would always want to follow me, but I would not let her because girls are afraid of the eels, especially the lamprey. My friends Christy, Timmy, and Tommy, had met me at the weir on the island bank, each of us clutching a table fork to hunt for the silver eels and eel fry under the rocks on the outgoing tide. All the time we kept a watchful eye out for the lamprey eel, which we knew would clamp onto your leg and suck all the blood out of it. Peter, who was bigger and older than us and used to have his goat run after us and butt us in his garden, had told us that the lamprey would suck all the blood out of one leg, and then when you fell down it would clamp onto your other leg and suck all the blood out of that one too. Then when the tide came in, you couldn't swim to the bank because your legs would be empty. So we were always on the lookout.

"Seanie, your mother is calling you." The chorus was from all three as I stood in a small pool with an eel impaled on my fork, and it wriggled free and fell back into the pool. I was sure my mother had frightened it.

Walking back over the slippery rocks to the grassy bank, I saw what I thought was an old kettle handle sticking out from under a big rock. I reached down and grabbed the brown, rusty handle, but to my surprise it slithered out of my grasp. Terror gripped me.

"Lamprey!" I shouted, as I leapt out onto a slippery rock and then fell backwards into the pool. I scrambled out and sure enough, the lamprey was in hot pursuit, making it to the bank.

All three of my friends, wide-eyed, sat panting. "Did he get you, Seanie?"

After checking my legs, I panted, "No," and walked slowly home with water dripping from my sodden short pants and leaving my barefoot prints in the field. I chastised the donkeys and horses grazing there, waving my fork at them as I made my way to our house on St. Ita's Street.

Katie, one of our neighbors, was standing at the gate, talking to my mother and handing her half an ounce of Halpins tea.

"How in the name of Jasus and his holy mother would we know the difference?" I heard my mother saying.

Her head nodding in approval, Katie said, "A truer word has never been spoken, Rosie."

"What we don't have we don't miss. Isn't that the truth, Katie?"

"Rosie, you can give me the half ounce when the wire boy comes with the telegram, but there is no rush. God love us all, Rosie. Tell me, how is Sonny doing in England? Do you ever think of going across yourself, Rosie?"

"Nosh at all, Katie. I buried my mother and father out at St. Patrick's and will be laid to rest with them, sure. If that gypsy tells me one more time that I will cross water after crossing her palm with a silver three-penny bit, I will stick it where I won't say in front of the children."

Looking down at me, my mother said, "In the name of the mother of God, how did your pants get wet? Go in the house and get them off." At which I dropped my wet pants and stood naked with only my ganzey pulled down to my knees.

Katie laughed and said, "God love him, Rosie, he is the picture of yourself," at which my mother burst out laughing.

"I will tell you, Katie, Sonny said he would rather be here out hunting rabbits with his friend Jack, but God love us, Katie, we can't live on rabbits, and feathery Bourke up in the Irishtown pays only a half penny for the skins. There's rabbit skins hanging to dry all over the house and the lot of them wouldn't pay for a couple of mackerel off Mary, the cat on Friday. Talking about Mary, did you hear what she was telling Seanie's friend, John F's grandmother up in Crosbie

Row? Well, I will tell you, Katie, I was wetting me knickers. She up and tells her that she was pulling her cart of mackerel up Nicholas Street on her way to the island in the drizzling rain and fog, when she heard the drone of a big flying boat overhead. She looks up, she says, and waves to the pilot—you know who I mean, Katie, the driver. Well, would you believe what she is up and is after telling the poor woman, and I'm not telling ye a word of a lie, may God strike me down dead, the pilot leans out of the window of the flying boat and says he to her, 'Would you tell me, missus, would I be anywhere near Foynes flying boat terminal?' At which she roared above the noise of the propellers, 'Go left and follow the River Shannon for a little bit and you will be there in no time at all.' At which he thanked her. She said that the good thing about it was the noise of the flying boat scared the daylights out of the cats following her. I tell you, Katie, I was crossing me legs.

"Katie, Sonny had a good job with the corporation; two brothers of his, Johnny and Pa Joe, are still there. I know he didn't like working on the rubbish lorry—he said the money in England was better and he is building ships as fast as the Germans are blowing them up. I don't mind, Katie, as long as he sends the two pounds now they are talking about putting the rent up to seven and six pence. I sometimes wish I was back in 2 Flag Lane up on Dominic Street, and Katie, I will tell you, if I was old enough when my two brothers and sisters left for America I would have sailed with them, but it wasn't meant to be. Meself, Kitty, Nora, and Paddy stayed with our mother and father in the lane. Mary and Peggy write to me, but I haven't heard from Jack or Tommy yet. They all went off to New York to work when I was only six, Katie."

I could hear the baby crying upstairs and Breeda saying, "Hush now," and singing to her, "Clap hands, clap hands till Daddy comes home. Cakes in his pocket for Frances alone."

My father would come home sometimes, and when he came the last time for the usual week's stay with us, he said to my mother, "Well now, and whose little child is this?"

She cried in anger, "I have been carrying three of your children for three long years. Rosaleen to April 1940, Michael to April 1941, and the baby to December 28ᵗʰ 1942, and you don't know who this child is? My God, it's a wonder you can remember Seanie and Breeda at all. What in the name of God are you thinking when you say that?" At which he left to return drunk that fateful day in our lives.

The times between his returning from England had been getting longer. I recall on one occasion, before Frances, the baby, was born, he came home and gave me two pennies, telling me to go and buy some sweets down at the shops. Before he returned to England, he promised to send me and Breeda a bike each. We were excited to know that we would be the only kids on the island who would have bikes, and after he went back to England we used to walk up to the railway station every day, hoping to ride the bikes back down to Island Field.

I was saying to Breeda, "When we take the bikes out of the tar paper, I will show you how to ride. We will ride all over Limerick— why they might even have new carbide lamps on them, and we will even be able to ride them at night. Wouldn't that be grand now?"

Her face lit up with the thought of it all. "Seanie Morrisey, you don't know how to ride a bike. I have not once in my life seen you on a bike."

"Sure, there's nothing to riding a bike at all," I said, hoping she would believe her big brother, but she was having none of it.

The bikes never arrived from England anyway, and we forgot about them, and we forgot our father's promise too.

On Saint Stephen's Day, we enjoyed roaming the streets chanting, "The wren, the wren the king of all birds, on St. Stephen's Day we caught in the furze. Up with the kettle and down with the pan. Give us a penny, and we will be gone, the wren, the wren, the wren." This pagan chant we sang each year as we went out to hunt the diminutive little bird and kill it, impaling it on a stick to parade in the streets, faces blackened with the ash from turf fire, and collecting a few pennies from the bemused neighbours.

As we sat on the old soldier's graveyard wall opposite "Dalcassin's" cabin, I was telling Timmy, whom we called Tiger, that I would be seven this year and couldn't wait to make my first Holy Communion where I would get more pennies than our father could afford. "When you become seven, Tiger, you have the use of reason. Father Costello told us in the convent."

"What's the use of reason, Seanie? I never was told about that."

"Well, when Father Costello comes to your class, he will tell you too. He said we become men at seven and have to go to confession if we commit a sin and tell the father all about the sin, and he will forgive us, and we can go to receive Holy Communion at Mass. If you commit a mortal sin you will go to Hell if you died, he said, but if you commit only venial sin, you go to Purgatory for a little bit. He said doing dirty things was a mortal sin."

Tiger asked me what dirty things would that mean, and I told him, "Things like doing cocky over water over the bank and the girls seeing us as we floated down the Shannon with our willies sticking out of the water. We have to wear costumes now."

"I don't have a costume."

"I don't either, Tiger. Jimmy [whom we called Pigeon] and Tommy or Christy or even John don't have one. I am going to cut the sleeves off me ganzey and put a safety pin in the neck and tie a string around me waist."

"Your mother will kill you, Seanie Morrissey," said he.

"If she does, I won't go to Hell because I will be wearing my costume, and St. Vincent de Paul will give me another ganzey to wear for school," I told him.

"Come and listen to me story, Molly Bawn. I am bound for death or glory, Molly Bawn. Sure, I listened to the army where no more those eyes could harm me. Ah, they'd kill me while they charmed me, Molly Bawn." The still air quivered while a tepid rain dampened our ganzies in that moist evening air as we heard Mr. McMahon singing while staggering past us. He was being held up by Mr. Roche, both

11

their faces as black as coal. They carried off the ships down at the docks, and there were white streaks from the rain running down their faces.

"Good night, Mr. McMahon, Mr. Roche!" we shouted from the wall.

"And who would you two soldiers be now?" Mr. McMahon said as he approached us.

"Seanie Morrissey and Timmy Garvey, Mr. McMahon," we told him.

"Sure, I know them," said Mr. Roche. "They're my son's friends, and shouldn't you two be at home instead of sitting here on the graveyard wall?"

"Fodder, would that be Rosie Plunkett's boy?" asked Mr. McMahon.

"It is, Gurkey."

"Well, I will tell you, Fodder, that woman can sing a song. She sure can sing."

I remembered my mother singing in the contest for ten shillings at the Thomond Cinema up on Nicholas Street when I was only four years of age. She stood on the stage in the lights as her black sequined dress sparkled. She won the ten shillings for singing, "You'll never know just how much I love you. You'll never know just how much I care, and if I tried, I still couldn't hide my love for you. You ought to know for haven't I told you so, a million or more times. You went away, and my heart went with you. I speak your name in my every prayer, and if there's some other way to prove that I love you, I swear I don't know how. You'll never know if you don't know now."

I suppose she missed our father, who was over in England working, because she said before she sang that it was for Hambone, the nickname he was called.

"Good night now, young fellas, and tell your mother, Seanie, that I was after asking about her," said Mr. Roche as they staggered on their way starting to sing again.

"Tiger, I wonder why Mr. McMahon called Mr. Roche 'Fodder' and him calling Mr. McMahon 'Gurky,'" I asked.

"I heard my father telling Mr. Fitzgerald that Mr. Roche was always farting, and he must have been eating the horse fodder, and Mr. Fitz saying that a farting horse never tires, that's why he is always working," Tiger said as a dog came running out of Copper Sporran's, the bonesetter's garden, barking at the men, with Gurky trying to kick it and calling it a mangy cos.

"Shawnee!" The ritualistic call came sailing through the evening air, and I remembered it was Friday and I had to have a bath before going to bed, the spoon of milk with Beecham's powder, and the spoon of horrible cod liver oil.

"I never mind the Beecham's, Tiger," I said as we walked barefoot up St. Ita's Street, "but I hate the cod liver oil."

"The same as meself, Seanie. It's awful. See you in the morning, Kayli," (my nickname), he said as he went in the gate.

On the kitchen floor in front of the turf fire was the zinc tub half full of dirty water with a bar of red carbolic soap and a rag floating in it. My mother was boiling a kettle of water on the cast-iron range, saying that the sods of turf were wet and calling the turf man a robber as the kids stood around the fire trying to dry off with a towel.

It will be dripping wet again, I thought. *It won't dry on the back of the chair in front of the smoldering sod of turf.*

"Tomorrow, Seanie, I want you to go up the Irishtown and ask the man in the furniture shop to let you please have some shavings off the floor for your poor mother for the fire. The shavings burn better," she said, after she packed the turf into the grate and stuck the broom handle down the middle to make a chimney, but it didn't last long burning. The sod of turf, even wet, would simmer all night and still be hot in the morning when we got up for school.

"I will, Mama," I replied as she poured the kettle of lukewarm water into the scum-ringed tub. The gas mantle began to flicker and the flame turned white as she told me to hurry up because she didn't have another penny to put in the gas meter.

When I went upstairs to bed, Breeda, Rosaleen, and Michael were already in the bed and the baby was in the cot that our father had made out of a toy box by the side where our mother would sleep. I put the empty bucket under the bed and climbed in next to Michael at the foot of the straw-filled mattress. A couple of the kids were scratching already with fleas, and it wouldn't be long before we all were, but we were used to them. They must have come with the straw from Cantillon's hay and straw shop at Charlotte Quay. No matter how many of them we caught and squashed with our thumbnails, blood squirting, the others took their place every night. The blanket on the window blocked out the light from across the road in front of the Tigers' house, and the other three grey blankets as well as the coat that my Aunt Mary had sent from America covered us all in bed. The little fire grate in the bedroom was not always lit unless we picked the coal from off the Dock Road that had fallen off horse and carts, but the other kids would also fight for the pieces. Pigeon said we could go behind McNamara's bakery on Mary Street and pick the coke out of the ashes, and if the other boys were there, we could go to Tubberty's down Athlunkard Street for some as well.

Most Sundays we would go over to Killeely, to our grandmother's house on Cregan Avenue for a "bish of dinner," my mother would say. She never came herself. Our grandmother was a very jovial woman with a big grin, showing her one tooth from under her black shawl pulled over her head as she tiptoed around the corner to Hassett's Cross public house before the afternoon dinner of usually pigs head, boiled cabbage, and potatoes. Around ten of us would all waiting for dinner; Aunt Maura's children, Teresa's, and Uncle Johnny's. We would be playing games out in the street and got called in about five at a time as the kitchen was too small and there were only five chairs. I was the eldest and would be asked to go around now to the snug and ask Nanna to come home for dinner. There were always four women sitting in the snug having their glass of porter, and the barman would slide the little wooden window aside and hand them their pints.

First Holy Communion Age 7

They weren't allowed to go in the bar where the men were always spitting in the sawdust on the floor, Nanna used to say, and that's why they sat in the snug sniffing their snuff. "The snuff stops the germs going up my nose from all the spitting," she said.

There was a ring of brown around her nostrils from all the sniffing. I would sometimes go to Clune's at 59 William Street for her sixpence worth of a half an ounce of black and white mixed. My mother would call her old Bridge instead of Bridgit, but I only called her Nanna or Mam, and we all loved her.

I had not known my grandfather John, as he died before I was born. Nanna said I was called after him and my second name after my other grandfather, Edward.

"But my name is Seanie," I told her.

"Sean is the same as John in Gaelic," she told me.

I didn't believe her. *Sean O, Muirgheasa is ainm dom,* the Christian brothers told me. Translated to English, which they hated to do, it was, "Sean Morrissey is my name," and so I learned as I started at Gerald Griffin Christian Brothers School in Creagh Lane.

Again, thinking back of sitting on the island bank looking at the rushing tide as the men on the weir were clubbing the salmon to death, memories flooded into my head of my father; my hanging on to his neck as we swam across the river at this very spot, he wearing his one-piece black swimming suit and I as naked as the day I was born. I thought, *What if I had lost my stranglehold grip from around his neck and was carried away by the rushing tide and into the weir gates? Would he have saved me?* I watched as a jackdaw landed on the weir railings, cawing at me, and again my thoughts were of the young jackdaw my father had brought home those long years ago as a pet for me.

"Look after him," he had instructed me, and he showed me how to feed him with the stick and bread and milk mixture. "If I cut his tongue with a sharp silver sixpence, he will talk for you," he said.

"Dad, I don't want him to talk," I replied, and he never did.

"Won't the fox eat him, Dad?" I queried, with the innocence of a three-year-old.

"He can't," he told me, "because he has no teeth."

I didn't know the fox was gummy. I later learned from my uncle Willy that dad had pulled out the fox's teeth with the pliers, and when he took the fox for walks on a lead, he would laugh when the fox jumped into his arms whenever threatened by the dogs that went for him. Years later, I wondered what ever happened to the fox. The jackdaw died up the chimney in the parlor. He had gone up there from the nest that I'd made for him in the grate. I put some paper in the grate and lit it to smoke him down, but he never came down.

At seven years of age I made my first Holy Communion while at St. Mary's Covent on the Island Road. Sister Philisitas had seen to it that I would be dressed in a suit and wearing stockings and shoes to kneel before God at the altar at St. Mary's. I looked grand, she said, and I was now the man of the house my mother told me, and God bless St. Vincent de Paul for the gifts of the suit, and we all said a prayer in the kitchen. My mother was looking at the soles of the shoes as I was kneeling on the floor with my hands clasped in front of me, Pigeon and I looking up at the ceiling while his mother, Mary, said to my mother, "Rosie, Pachy Brown won't take the shoes."

"And why not?" my mother said.

"The soles of the shoes have a stamp in the leather, and it says *CP*."

"And what in the name of God does that mean, Mary Cronin, at all?"

"Well, Rosie, Stella Sheedy told me that after her Babs made her first Holy Communion, and wasn't that last year, Pachy wouldn't take the shoes because he said that the stamp was *CP,* meaning 'can't pawn.' It's a wonder she hasn't told you herself, Rosie."

"Sure, I don't think that would have crossed her mind, Mary. She was having a hard-enough time herself as meself, what with her husband Matthew taking his hook like Sonny and leaving her with the three children. There's a curse on the Island Field, Mary. When

I go into Pachy's, I will let him have a piece of my mind because the stamp is *GP*, and that means 'Government Property' and not 'Can't pawn' at all at all. Next thing you know, she will be saying the label in the coat my sister Mary sent from America, which she only gives me five bob for, is foreign made. It's getting harder to get it out every week as you have noticed the wire boy cycling past our house lately. Sure, if it wasn't for that young girl Frances Hourigan minding the children for me while I worked up at the bakery, the coat would be sold from under me eyes for a couple of shillings. I called the baby after her and hope my Frances turns out as good as her. She is like one of me own, God love her."

Looking back, remembering the day I made my first Holy Communion, Father Costello had heard my confession, and I was only given three Hail Marys, three Our Fathers, and a Glory Be to God, for penance, while Pigeon and Tiger took longer saying their penance. I would have to ask them what penance they had got and why, what had they done? But I knew that they would not tell me their sins anymore. We had come to the use of reason. That Sunday we knelt at the altar with our tongues sticking out, forever it seemed, as we waited for Father Lee to put the Holy Communion on our parched tongues. My mouth was dry as the wafer itself when he eventually placed it saying, "This is my body and this is my blood." I opened one eye and looked at him as he stuck the holy wafer in my mouth. I blessed myself and still with my mouth open and the wafer stuck on my tongue, walked past Tommy, Christy, Whacker, Carroll, and all the gang, all dressed in St. Vincent de Paul suits. I could feel their eyes following me as I made my way past them up the aisle to where I knelt and tried to swallow the Communion. I was frightened to let my teeth touch the body of Jesus because it would be a sin. And even if you are hungry and are tempted to eat it, you must not, Sister Philisitas had told us. I pulled my tongue in and tried to swallow it, but it got stuck in my throat, and I panicked. Choking and now my face turning red, I coughed, and it now got stuck on the roof of my mouth. I wriggled my tongue trying to dislodge it, but it wouldn't move. My Aunt Maura, seeing the commotion from the back of the church, came and took me by the hand, led me to the entrance, and with her open hand scooped up the holy water from the font and had me drink it, washing the Holy Communion down and away from my teeth, to my relief.

I was happy to leave St. Mary's that day, visiting all the family and being given a few pennies from each of them, remarking that I was looking lovely in the new suit and the shining new shoes. The next day, the suit was hanging in Pachy's up in Irishtown, but the shoes stayed with me until worn out in the following months.

"Your good-for-nothing father will be happy to know you're back on your feet again," my mother said, and started laughing at that. "Go over to old Bridge and tell her to tell her son to send you a pair of shoes to put on your feet. Tell her to tell him to wrap them up with the two bikes," she said with some sarcasm. But I never did tell Nanna that Mam had called her old Bridge, nor did I ask for the shoes to be wrapped with the bikes that Breeda and I had long forgotten about. My bare feet had hardened like leather, not like they were when I'd jumped off the stable into the horse manure at the back of Charlie's house, the big nail in the old horseshoe going into my foot, festering, and I being sick in bed with the fever. If it wasn't for my Uncle Willy giving me a shilling, I thought that I would have never got well at all. He said it was a magic shilling to make me better.

"We can't afford to feed the greyhound," my mother said, "and the island has dogs running all over the place, most with the mange. We have to put him down as your father has sent word from England. We don't want him to starve to death, now do we, Seanie?"

"But Mama, he can have some of my dinner, can't he?"

"That's not dog food, Seanie," Breeda said.

"Shut up you, giddy biddy," I said back.

"That will be enough out of you now, Seanie Morrissey. Your sister has St. Vitus's dance, and that is no way to talk to your sister at all. You're old enough to stop talking like that now, what with all the names you call one another."

"Well she calls me 'Jeff,' and calls Rosaleen 'a bag of nails.'"

"Well, Seanie, you call Michael 'Mutt' and the baby 'Odd Eyes.'"

"Well, that's because she has a brown eye, and the other one is blue."

"Enough," my mother said. "In the morning take Tuppence up to the cruelty man's and let him know your father said to put him down."

"Why do they call me a bag of nails, Mama?" Rosaleen asked.

"Because you are always crying that you're hungry," I quipped.

"I said that will be enough, and I won't tell you again," my mother said. "Up the stairs and into the bed the lot of you. I'll be up shortly and read ye all a letter from your Aunt Mary."

"Can I give Tuppence the sheepshead out of the pot, Mama?"

She took out the last cup of soup and let me take the sheepshead out to Tuppence in the shed. I gave him the sheepshead and gave him a hug, going back inside and up the stairs, dejected,

My mother came up and asked us to be quiet and stop kicking one another in the bed, or she wouldn't read us the letter. There was a candle on a saucer by the bed, and she took the letter out of the bag of letters she kept under the bed and started to read it, leaning away toward the candle.

"My dear Rosie," Mother started.

My mother told us that Breeda was only one and myself two when the letter was written, and then she went on.

My dear Rosie,

I hope you will excuse me for not writing to you before now, but somehow, I put it off from one day to another, and now it's months before I drop you a few lines. Well, how are you, and how's Nora and Paddie? I suppose asking you after such a long time won't do you any good, but I am sorry. Now the children are all gone back to school, and I have a little time to sit down. They are home all summer. They don't have any school in the summer here. Georgan, she is twelve now, and she's always talking about you, Nora, and Paddie. And Kitty, of course, my own Kitty is ten and a half, and she's a big girl too. And then Peter, he is eight and a half, and he wants to write to Paddie. He thinks Paddie is my little brother. And the baby, she is seven. Nedra is her name. I called her after my father. Well, have you heard from Peg? I haven't seen her in a long time. She was building a house in Huntington, Long Island. The last time we went to see her, but I haven't gone to see her lately because our car needs fixing. And George, my husband, didn't have the spare time to fix it. As for Jack, I haven't seen him in years or Tommie, so I guess we are just a grand family. I heard an Irish play from Dublin over the radio last night. It was good. It's wonderful to be able to hear right from Ireland. The kiddies were delighted.

The candle began to flicker and I was the only one still awake as my mother's hand holding the letter dropped while I struggled to keep my eyes open.

The next morning, walking to Creagh Lane School, Christy joined me as I passed his house, and Pigeon and Tiger ran to catch up to us. We had to be in the yard before the hand bell that Brother McGuire used to ring. If you weren't and you were late, he used to hide behind the door to the yard and beat you across the legs with the leather, yelling that you were lazy and not fit to get the bun and milk at break time, and you could say goodbye to your breakfast. By the time we got to school, they all knew of my rich family in America and all my cousins there, who had a radio and a motorcar.

I came home from school early that day because my mother had given me a halfpenny to put in the poor black babies in Africa box, and when you put a halfpenny in the box you were allowed to leave school a half hour early. That unforgettable day, I placed the rope around Tuppence's neck as tears welled in my eyes. He looked at me with sadness in his eyes as if he knew what I was about to do and licked my face, like he understood. I was to carry his picture with me for the rest of my life. My mother said not to be sad as Tuppence would be better off in Heaven where he would be well fed with all the rashers, backbones, eye bones, pig's heads, sheep heads, and pig tails to eat to his heart's content.

"In fact," she said, "as you go past Mrs. Callahan's offal shop, you will see all that meat in the window." She stroked the greyhound's back, and I thought I saw a tear. Walking slowly to the cruelty man's yard, my heart thumped in my chest, and I felt hatred for what my father had told my mother to have me do. Hadn't my mother said I was the master of the house? And I was nine years old too. Eventually, with a heavy heart, Tuppence and I came to the entrance of the yard. And with a trembling hand, I knocked on the door to be greeted by a big balding giant of a man. He looked down at the greyhound and me, telling us to come into the yard. He led us to a smaller yard and turned on the water tap. I wondered what he was doing. Was he going to give Tuppence a bath? The cold water ran into my bare feet and continued down the drain that would make its way to the Shannon River. He left us standing there as he made his way back to the house to return a few minutes later carrying a big shining gun in his hand. It was bigger than my grandmother's.

He closed the yard door behind him. "Your mother told me that you would bring Tuppence," he said as he took the rope out of my shaking hand and tied it to a hook on the wall. "He will be better off in Heaven," he said. "He is very thin. Will you look at his bones, Seanie? And he is getting old. Will you want to leave now, son? He won't feel any pain at all."

"No I want to stay with him, mister." I said.

"Well, close your eyes and say a little prayer for him."

"Hail Mary, full..."and BANG. There was a terrible ringing in my ears as I opened my eyes to watch Tuppence slump to the concrete floor. The water ran red and lukewarm between my toes, my heart thumping in my chest as I stared at the gaping hole in my dog's forehead, his tongue hanging out. I couldn't cry or speak for days. The ringing of the gunshot was to accompany me for eternity, it seemed, as I walked from the yard with the piece of rope that the cruelty man had handed me, leading me out the door and giving me a pat on the head for being a brave boy. He said, "Tuppence is in Heaven now."

Eventually I told Breeda what had happened, and she cried, saying that our father didn't care about us or the dog anymore, and he was always away in England anyways. Upstairs in the bedroom, coal that had fallen off the carts on the Dock Road was burning in the fire grate as the five of us huddled around it to keep warm. The bed was covered with an old grey blanket, the room in complete darkness except for the dancing flames lulling us into a trancelike state as we hoped our mother would hurry home from work with fish and chips from Marcella's and our weekly bottle of Guinness, which she said cleared the blood. In my pocket was a big bullet that I had found in the cubbyhole above the coalhole in the kitchen. Our father must have hidden it there with the ferret bags and the revolver that the bullet did not fit as it was too big and cut into my thumb as I cocked it to put the bullet in. Fiddling with the bullet in my pocket, I wondered what would happen if I threw it in the fire. Without a second thought, I tossed it in. Some time passed and nothing happened as we sat on the floor watching an orange flame licking the big bullet casing. All of a sudden, there was a flash and a loud explosion as a hail of hot coals flew right over our heads. Breeda and Rosaleen screamed. With a big grin on his face, Michael yelled, "Do it again, Seanie!" over the screaming. As the red-hot coals landed on the blanket covering the straw mattress, little fires started to burn all over it.

Oh God, I thought. *What can I tell my mother and Aunt Frances? My mother will kill me.*

The baby was howling for her mama.

"I will go and tell Auntie Frances and tell her about you, Seanie," yelled Breeda.

"You can't go out, Breeda," I told her. "Mama said we are not to go down the stairs at night."

"And why not, Seanie Morrissey?"

"Because Mama said so, and you could fall down, giddy biddy."

"I'll tell Mama you're calling me names too, *Jeff.*"

I had heard our mother telling Stella Fitz that the only good thing about the corporation house from the lanes was that we had a lavatory next to the kitchen, but she was saying that she was frightened of the children coming down at night. "Sure, the old bucket under the bed is handy, Stella," she said. "Some of the stairs are missing, chopped up for fire. Some made into little bundles and sold for a couple of pence out of the pram by Seanie and Breeda." Our mother had said that her friend Joe would fix the stairs soon, so we wouldn't have to walk like crabs going up to bed and hop like fleas coming down.

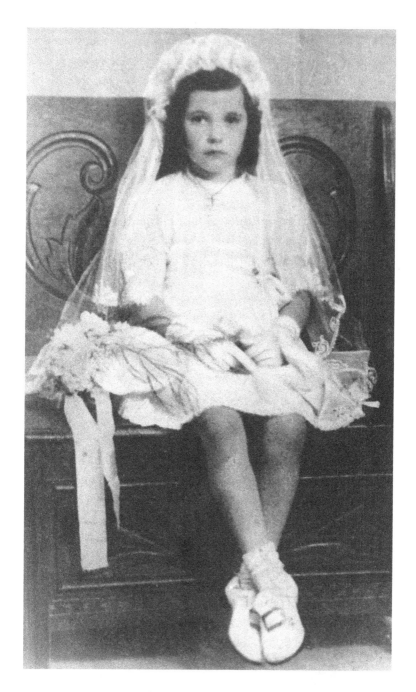

"What in the name of the suffering Jasus happened in this bedroom tonight?" our mother roared when she came upstairs with a big bag of fish and chips and two bottles of Guinness in her old coat pockets. "Can't leave ye for two minutes and ye nearly burn the house down around me. What have ye done?"

"Seanie done it, Mama, and he called me 'giddy biddy' again," Breeda said, her ash-covered face streaked with tears.

"Seanie Morrissey, how many times have I told you? What happened to the blanket and the room full of smoke?" Mother said as she pulled down the other blanket from the window and opened the window. "In the future, Frances Hourigan will have to watch ye till I get home from St. Patrick's Bakery. God knows I'm only there two days a week, and still by the time I get home from Catherine Street, ye have the house wrecked."

"Mama, I didn't know the old bullet would do that. I thought it would only burn with the coal," I pleaded as she sat on the bed crying, her face drained as she looked at the five of us, her tears dripping onto the newspaper holding the fish and chips and Rosaleen trying to wipe her tears away.

"Seanie has made you cry again," said Breeda, giving me a slap on the head.

I bowed my head in silence as my mother separated the chips into five little heaps on the pieces of the *Echo* newspaper and added pieces of fish to each. She poured out our weekly cup of Guinness into the condensed milk cans. Bellies filled, we fell asleep one by one on the burned bed.

One day, our mother's old coat was hanging on the nail at the backdoor as she was washing and scrubbing the clothes on the washboard in the backyard, taking one piece at a time, wringing out the water, and hanging them on the clothesline to dry, which they never did because it always seemed to be drizzling rain. She was saying to Stella, "No wonder they all have snotty noses," laughing and adding that she hoped the rag-and-bone man would not pass by and see the clothes, for he would give her a balloon for the lot of them.

I reached up and put my hand into her coat pocket searching for one of the boiled sweets that she put in the tea because of the shortage of sugar and because she had sold the coupons from the ration book a long time ago. I felt a coin and took it out. It was a shilling. It looked old and had soap on it. She must have forgotten about it, but I couldn't tell her, so I put it back.

The next time I put my hand into the pocket, the shilling was gone, and I thanked God that I had not kept it, or she would have killed me all together. I was forever upsetting her as it was, with my mooching from school, thieving, begging, and running away from home. This time, all I pulled out was a piece of paper. It was like a telegram, and I read it in the lavatory, sliding the bolt shut. The heading said:

London Midland and Scottish Railway Company
Irish Traffic Manager's Office
North Wall Station
Dublin

In your reply please
DPW7/2763
4TH September 1947

Ms. Breeda Morrison
76 St. Ita's
Island Field
Limerick

Dear Madam,

One Cycle

With further reference to the above cycle on hand here for customs requirements, to enable me to proceed with the clearance, I shall be glad if you will please let me have your remittance for two pound fifteen shillings and four pence duty assessed on this cycle, as soon as possible. Please quote my reference as above in your reply and oblige.

Yours faithfully,

For A.J BROUGHTON

This consignment is detained on account of customs, government, or local regulations. The company accordingly holds the same as warehousemen subject to their usual charges.

My mouth hung open having now realized that my father had only sent Breeda a bike, but where was it? Two pounds fifteen and four pence was a lot of money. I knew as my mother had been telling Stella that she was having an awful time with rent every week and was afraid that we would be evicted as the rent man said. I put the telegram and the shilling back in the pocket and walked out the front door, running away in anger.

A couple of days later, I decided to return. I had been hiding out in the bushes on the Ennis Road. My bed had been newspapers with twigs stuck in the corners, holding them to stop them blowing away, and covering myself at night with others.

"But the cold and wet was the reason for my return and not hunger," I had told my mother. She was wondering where I was as was Guard White. I had been begging at the rich people's houses, asking for a penny or a piece of bread, but I didn't tell her about me running after the bread and bun van or finding the telegram in her pocket. She would have killed me for going in her pockets, but I told Christy about the bread and buns.

This is a picture taken by the National Geographic Magazine of Creagh Lane school during Milk and Bun (break) time. When the picture was first published c. 1941, later in Denis O'Shaughnessy's book, it caused tremendous excitement. ⌐ This particular copy of the picture is owned by Noel Buckley and submitted by Gui

I saw the horse and cart trotting down the road and ran after it, and then I pulled out the wood peg on the back doors, and the bread and cake trays tumbled out on me. A tray landed on my big toe and I grabbed a cottage loaf in my arms, running as fast as my legs could carry me, my chest heaving with excitement, and my big toe throbbing as I made it back to my den in the bushes. I looked back at the horse and cart and bread and cakes were still falling out all over the road. I found a condensed milk can in the field near the horse trough and put the ice cream that I had bought with a penny that I'd begged for in it and some water, and it looked just like milk, but not like the creamy milk that we got at school, and it tasted rusty. I tore the cottage loaf apart and ate half of it before going to the houses again farther up Ennis Road. I got sixpence halfpenny. One lady gave me three farthings and a piece of chicken that I hid in the bushes at the bottom of her garden. It was wrapped in newspaper. And I continued begging. When I came back to pick up the piece of chicken, I watched a mangy dog devouring it.

"But there was nothing that I could do," I told Christy.

My mother beat me with the sweeping brush for running away, but I was glad to be home anyway. And, I was still wondering where Breeda's bike was, as I made my way the following morning to Creagh Lane. I knew that I would get a hiding from Brother McGuire, but Whacker had told me that a horse hair or two laid across your palm would take the sting of the leather.

Creagh Lane School loomed in front of me as the coal man's horse and cart trundled up Nicholas Street. The big horse, blinkered, stopped now and again without a word of command from the coal man and moved again as the half-hundred-weight bags of coal were lifted off on the coal man's back, to stop again at the next regular customer's door.

"At ten shillings a hundred weight, very few can afford it," my mother had said.

I walked up to the horse and patted his neck. "Good boy," said I, as I pulled a hair from his mane. He snorted, throwing his head up in protest, but I had the hair. I placed the hair across the palm of my right hand, holding it tightly with my thumb, and said to myself, "Well, Baldy, here I come."

"It didn't work," I told Pigeon and John Fahy as we stood outside the bun and milk shop on Mary Street later. "He gave me six on both hands, and I felt all of them," I said, as I was shoving the bun into my hungry mouth with swollen hands. They were still tingling, and I had to use both hands to hold the bottle of milk. "I only had the hair on my right hand, but when the leather was coming down on it, I dropped my hand a little bit, and the hair must have fallen off. So for dropping my hand, he gave me six more on my other hand. I hate Baldy," I said through a halo of rich, creamy milk clinging to my mouth. I put the bottle down on the ground and gingerly picked up what remained of the dry bun.

There were some men and they had a camera on a pole telling us to gather together so they could take our picture next to the bun and milk shop by Broderick's chemist shop. They said they were from the *National Geographic*, but we didn't know what they were talking about as we all stood and some boys sat facing the camera.

When I got home, I told my mother that I might be in the pictures as the men were from America, and my mother said the Americans call them movies and not pictures at all, telling me to get my hands out of my pockets and to run up to Mullane's for some packet and tripe for dinner. She said she would give me a halfpenny to buy seaweed (dillisk) or periwinkles from Sparling's. I loved the seaweed. I ran as fast as I could to Squeeze Gut Lane, and Spoons Sheehan took the money that was wrapped in a piece of paper and handed me the packet and tripe in some newspaper. I asked my mother what the packet and tripe was made of as we all loved it, and she told us that tripe was from the stomach of the sheep, and the packet was spiced blood. I gave the others a sideways glance and could see disbelief in their eyes also. Later, I heard Breeda and Rosaleen saying, "Yuck," as they talked about it outside while playing with their spinning tops. I had often wondered why the slaughterhouse man on the back Island Road saved the sheep's blood in the tray after cutting their throats with the knife. It tasted good at supper. Their bladders were no good for a football, though. Only the cows' bladders blew up big enough, and we had to have a lot of breath to blow them up, but they smelled after a couple of days, and we had to get another one or a pig's bladder from Matterson's.

Rooting through the ashes behind McNamara's bakery shop with ropes tied around our waists, Pigeon and I picked the best pieces of coke that we could find, stuffing the warm coal waste inside our ganzies. The grey ash covered our half-naked bodies, but we were warm, and the coke would be a welcome change from the water-soaked turf that just simmered away on the fire all night and gave out very little heat at all.

Our ganzies bulging with the coke, we stopped on the Thomond Bridge to feel the imprint of the bishop's lady's fingers on the blue/

granite parapet where her ghost was said to linger, just to show we were not afraid of her. When a hand touched my shoulder, my heart almost stopped with fright as I looked at Pigeon and saw his hands were on the parapet. I turned slowly to see a lady holding a camera with a smile spread across her face.

"Would you mind if I take your picture?" she said in an American accent.

"We don't mind, missus," Pigeon replied with a smile on his blackened face.

The lady was laughing as she took the picture and she gave us two shillings each. We wondered if she was nuts as we ran down the strand and into Island Field.

We were to learn a few months later why she was laughing when she took the picture. A letter arrived from the USA, and in it was the photo with a note: "From the lady who took your picture." The photo showed the end piece of rope tied around my waist hanging down in front of my flies. Our mother was killing herself laughing and saying we were becoming film stars with all the pictures being taken of us by the Americans.

I wanted to tear up the picture before anyone else saw it, but my mother put the one I got away somewhere in the house to show my Uncle Paddy and Aunt Kitty and Nora, and Pigeon wouldn't give me his one and told me he would show it to the gang. I told him I would punch him in the nose if he did, and he never did as far as I knew. I wouldn't have punched him in the nose anyway even if he did. He was my mate.

At the Corcanree dump, where the ground was always simmering continuously, an eternal burning ember of human waste and carcasses and bloated bodies of domestic animals hummed to an orchestra of bluebottle flies and a never-ending chorus of screaming, mostly one-legged seagulls. They danced to the tune of the dog-sized rats, lifting and landing as the rats scurried from one bloated carcass to the next, paying no particular attention to me and the other scavengers as we rooted through the fresh dumped loads of waste. My bare feet were warmed by the heat; feet that were becoming hardened like well-hammered leather. I searched for discarded toys and anything else of value but rarely found anything of value at all. In fact, I never did. On my way home with the rope tied around my waist holding the body of a ragdoll in my ganzey for the baby, pieces of coal that had fallen off the horse and carts were like ice cubes against my bare stomach. They soon warmed, though, not like the coke from behind the baker's shop, which was always warm, but any fuel was welcomed in the bedroom grate.

"You haven't been to school again, Seanie, have you?" Breeda said, as I undid the knot in the rope, letting the pieces of coal drop to the floor along with the coal-black rag doll.

"Who wants to know?" says I.

"Well, Guard White was here looking for you," she said with a smug look on her face, and at the same time picking up the blackened rag-doll. "You dropped your black baby," she laughed.

"You're a liar, Breeda Morrissey, and I don't care anyway. I'm not frightened by him," I said.

She said, "I'll tell Mama when she gets home, Seanie Morrissey."

"I'm shivering in me boots," says I, looking down at my bare feet, and we both started laughing.

"You're a gom, *Jeff.*"

"If you don't stop calling me and Michael Mutt and Jeff, I'll call you giddy, biddy."

That night, after we all went to bed, we listened to our mother scrubbing the clothes in the tub on the washboard, singing to herself every now and again, and I thought I heard her sob in between. I thought that the new job at the hotel wasn't paying her enough money to pay the rent, for I had heard her telling Aunt Nora, while we were down at St. Munchin Street, that she'd had to pawn everything in order to try and catch up with the rent, or we would be evicted by Christmas.

Aunt Nora was after telling her that Uncle Mikey was having to look for another job himself as the money he was getting wasn't enough, and she said the money of Aunt Kitty's husband, Timmy Hourigan, didn't even make it in the door, and poor Aunt Kitty had to work up in Pery Square at the library, looking after the boiler as well as cleaning it and the library. "Sure, Rosie," she said, "little Rita and Mary had to help her with it, and they were missing school as well. There's no one to turn to at all."

My mother said that Mary and Peggy might send her a couple of American dollars, but Aunt Nora said that they were too far away in America, and they had family of their own to look after.

"The rent book was in Sonny's name," my mother said.

"And wouldn't you think Pa Joe or Johnny would tell the Limerick Corporation that the rent is too high, but all I hear is that Pa Joe is the foreman and he's hiring men from all over Limerick—men that as soon as he hires them steal the shovels and brushes and sell them. Enough said," Aunt Nora said.

I couldn't sleep in the bed thinking of the sadness that our mother was suffering.

"Uncle Paddy is not well," I heard my mother tell Nora. Aunt Mary and Uncle Tommy in America were thinking of bringing him to America, she said. "What about Kathleen and the children, Noreen, John, and Madge?"

"She is like us, Rosie. She won't leave her mother on her own."

Uncle Paddy and Aunt Kathleen lived above the fish and chips shop on Nicholas Street, and Uncle Paddy would miss days working at the blacksmith shop in upper Denmark Street. He had TB and was thinking of taking a job away from the hard work, I heard my aunt Kathleen telling my mother. "There was a job he was offered pasting up the posters, and all he had to do was to carry a bucket of paste, a brush, and the posters. But Rosie," she said, "The money that they paid wasn't very much and I asked Mela Marsella to give me a little time to pay the rent."

I was sitting at the table watching my mother counting out two shillings from the sixpences, three-penny bits, and also pennies that she got from the gas man after he read the meter in the kitchen. I looked at the rent book and saw arrears was four pound, sixteen and three pence and asked my mother where we were going to live if we got moved out for not being able to pay the money every week.

"If Aunt Kathleen can't pay the four shillings a week for the little room over the chip shop, how could you pay eight shillings a week, Mama?" I said.

"Will you whisht now, Seanie. You are giving me a headache," she replied. "And you are upsetting the children."

"I'm not children, Mama," the baby said. "I'm six," as the four of them with their chins resting on the table watched.

"Are we leaving the house like Seanie said, Mama?" Breeda asked.

"See what I mean? Now stop it. We are not being evicted. I will have the rent money. You go outside and play, and Seanie, put your Wellingtons on those feet."

"But, Mama, they hurt," I said. "They are too small."

But she insisted, and I hobbled out into the front street to join the boys, who were playing our favourite game of cross-over-water under the Garvey's street light, before I pulled off the rubber boots.

The next day it was drizzling rain and the mud was squelching between my toes as I pondered whether I should go to school again today or mooch to go out on the Ennis Road. I thought that I could go up and see Uncle Paddy at the blacksmith shop and watch him heat and hammer out the horseshoes on the big anvil. He would let me swing on the handle of the bellows, helping him fire up the coke as the sparks flew like fireflies to the roof above, sparkling as his big hammer hit on the still red-hot horse shoes while the nervous horses shivered in anticipation. There was the smell of the melting hooves as he fitted the hot metal shoes and smoke filled the air.

I decided to go out to the Ennis Road first and beg for some money and bread. I hadn't been there for a couple of weeks. I begged until I had enough to buy a kid goat, and I also was given some cooked meat and pieces of bread. I took the bread and meat home and put it in the bread bin in the backyard and went up the Irishtown. Gypsies haggled over the price of saddle-back horses, donkeys, and ginnets, which I knew were more than likely strays that had somehow become attached to their caravans as they roamed the county, mending pots and pans, making tea cups out of condensed milk cans, or telling fortunes after having their palms crossed with silver; the usual three-penny bit.

Goats wandered around the straw-strewn street, and the smell of urine mingled with the recognizable cocktail of Guinness, porter, fish and chips, and vomit. Patchy Brown's pawnshop with the three brass balls hanging outside just a hundred yards away was doing a roaring business. He would take in anything; the men's Sunday suits, which they would take out on a Friday and put back again on the Monday and pay to get their work pants and jackets back out for work; wedding rings; boots; shawls; and bibs. I went in, had a good look around, and wondered if he had Breeda's bike, but I didn't see a girl's bike at all.

On Saturday, the market was teeming with farmers buying and selling cabbage plants, potatoes, geese, chickens, kid goats, carrots, parsnips, and eggs, while outside on the walls were clothes hanging on carts; discarded clothes that even Pachy wouldn't take in. I wandered around asking the farmers if they needed help with their purchases and would be asked to carry the bundles of plants, etc., to their horse-drawn carts and would be given a couple of shillings on a good day. Some of the farmers were more generous than others, and I would give our mother the money, and Michael began to call me Dad.

I was told by our mother that I could buy a kid goat with the sixpence I had. She wanted to know where I'd gotten the sixpence, and I told her from the market, and she said I could keep the goat in the back garden where the weeds grew high, but that was all I would get. "Do you understand me?" she said.

"I do, Mama," I said as I left the house with a big grin across my face.

I could rob Peter's father's garden where he grows turnips, and the goat would be eating well, I thought. Peter was always having me and Christie being the horses and he himself the driver on the cart up-and-down St. Ida's street, and we didn't like being the horses all the time, so I would get my own back and rob their turnips.

The goat was white and only a few months old but it didn't live very long, and I got a taste for the turnips myself. Soon I was robbing potatoes as well from Mr. Garvey's front garden, but I never told Timmy.

The tables and chairs were gone from the kitchen. There were bags filled with everything, and I saw the rent book on the floor behind the front door. The mattress was gone off the bed upstairs and only the iron bed frame remained. Breeda, Rosaleen, and Michael were sitting on the stairs when I came home, the baby sleeping in Breeda's arms, and she herself falling asleep.

"Where's Mama?" I said.

"She is taking us to the new house when she comes home," Rosaleen said back to me.

"What new house?" I said as I picked up the rent book off the floor.

"We don't know," Michael replied. "We are hungry."

I went across the road to Mrs. Nash and asked her for the old mouldy bread from her bread bin, which she usually gave us, and I scraped the green mould off with a knife. There were dried-out tea leaves by the sink in our kitchen. We had used them about two times, so they were still able to brew, and I boiled the pan of water on the gas stove and made some weak tea. The gas light was still lit in the kitchen, but the mantel had a hole in it and showed a white flame instead of blue. As I looked at the rent book page seeing why we had to move, Michael and Rosaleen ate the bread and sipped the hot tea from the condensed milk cup tins. Breeda said she wasn't hungry and only wanted to sleep.

Tenant's Rent Book.

Name: Michael Morrison 1947
Residence: 76 Saint Ita's Street.
Rent per week: 5/6 [crossed out and 7/3 put in its place], payable in advance on Monday of each week.

Month and Date, Rent due. Cash received. By Who Received, When Received, Arrears.

Brought Forward	Pounds Shillings and Pence		P-S-P	4/ 15/ 0	
March 31	5 – 0 - 6	7 - 0	O/C	4/4	4 - 13 - 6
April 6	4 – 19 – 6	7 - 0	32	12/4	4 - 12 – 0
14	4 – 17 – 6	7 - 0	32		
21	4 – 16 – 16				
May 5	4 – 15 =	6 – 0	32	10/5	4 – 9 – 0
12	4 – 16 – 6	6 – 0	32	17/5	4 – 8 - 6
19	4 – 15 – 9	8 – 0	32	24/5	4 – 7 – 9
26	4 – 15 =				
June 2	5 – 2 – 3	15 – 6	gz	5/6	4 – 6 - 9
9	4 – 14 =				

16	5 – 1 – 3	15 – 0	gz	5/7	4 – 5 – 3
23	4 – 13 - 6				
June 30	5 – 0 – 9	15 – 0	gz	5/7	4 – 5 – 9
7/7	4 – 13 - 0				
14/7	5 – 0 – 3	15 – 0	gz	19/7	4 – 5 – 3
21/7	4 – 12 – 6	7 – 6	gz	24/7	4 – 5 - 0
28/7	4 – 12 - 3				
Aug 4	4 – 19 – 6	7 – 6	gz	5/8	4 – 12 - 0
11	4 – 19 - 3				
18	5 – 6 – 6	16 – 0	gz	22/8	4 – 10 – 6
25	4 – 17 – 9	8 – 0	30/8	4-9-9	
Sept 1	4 – 17 – 0	8 – 0	gz	5/9	4 – 9 - 0
8/9	4 – 16 – 3				4 – 16 – 3
15/9	5 – 3 – 6				5 – 3 - 6
22/9	5 – 10 – 9	5-10-9			
29/9	5 – 18 - 0				5 – 18 - 0
Oct 6	6 – 5 – 3				6 – 5 - 3
13/10	6 – 12 - 6				6 – 12 - 6
20/10	6 – 19 – 9				6 – 19 – 9

My tea was cold when I finished looking at the rent book and trying to make sense of the figures. I could see that the rent wasn't marked in for the last four weeks and knew we were being evicted, but where we would go, I didn't know. Maybe to Aunt Nora's on St. Munchin's Street. Maybe our mother was there.

I remember it was a cold October night, rain drizzling. We had fallen asleep when the front door opened. It was our mother, shaking her wet coat in the hall, and a man was with her. She told us he was a friend and was called Joe and was helping us move to the new house on Robert Street, across from the market.

The pram was in the hall. She and Joe, her boyfriend, put the rest of the stuff in it, and she put the sleeping baby on top of some of the clothes. We closed the door behind us as we left Island Field in the middle of the night, leaving the iron bed frame still bolted together up in the bedroom. I still had the rent book in my hand as we arrived at the abandoned butcher shop at 10 Robert Street next to Mossy Reidy's coal yard, which I knew very well. No coal ever fell off Mossy's horse and carts.

The mattress was filled with fresh straw and lying on the concrete floor, and the big shop window was covered with a blanket; a blanket that wasn't needed for the dirt on the window would have sufficed. There was also a big fireplace, cold and uninviting, in a corner of the flagstone floor. It wasn't long before the rats were making us a visit at night.

"The only place that they could be coming in would be down the chimney," Joe said, after I killed one coming on to the bed with an old butcher knife one night. I had found the rusty butcher's knife when we moved in, and kept it under the mattress. The others were sleeping when I heard the scratching farthest away from me. I was nearest the front door in the bed. I lit a match and saw the rat in the corner by Frances. I put my hand under the mattress and in an instant threw the knife, pinning him to the damp wall. Rosaleen screamed, waking the others. Our mother heard all about it when she came in, smelling of the drink, and she said that we were not to tell anyone about it as we would be evicted from the shop.

It was becoming easier to steal, and I mooched more often. Instead of begging, I stole sweets and bread out of vans, oranges from the warehouse, and apples from Gus Hanley's orchard. I worked at a yard next to the market. For holding the chaff bags at the threshing machine or sorting the boxes of live chickens for transport, my pay would be a chicken. They were chickens that my mother said were like rubber because they were so old. She would boil them on the fire after taking out the coal bags that were stuffed up the chimney during the day. She was afraid that the chimney would catch fire like it had in St. Ita's Street when Breeda and Rosaleen were trying to make chocolate out of cocoa and water when she was out.

I went to school some days, but I was getting beatings more often for mooching. I had been up to the *Limerick Leader* newspaper office on O'Connell Street and got a job of selling the newspaper. For every twelve I sold around town, I got the thirteenth one for myself; two pennies worth. I was after selling twenty-two and on my way down to Island Field to see if Pigeon and Christy wanted to go to the pictures at the Thomond, although it cost sixpence to get in. Jack or Maxi on the door taking the tickets would let you in for two pence if you showed them two fingers.

We always stooped down so the woman who took the money and gave you the ticket would not see us as we gave Jack or Maxi the two-finger sign, got the nod, and ducked as we gave them the money and one of us crept in. The one who got in then went down by the front wooden benches and when the lights went down, opened the exit emergency door a bit and let the others in. After you let the others in, you left the bench near the door. That bench was always empty after the lights went down. You had to be quick and sneak into one of the seats as Jack or Maxi would come around with their flash lights looking for whoever sneaked in, and if they caught you, you were hauled out by the ear and given a kick in the arse from them, and they wouldn't let you in again for the two pence for a long time. Then you would only have the Tivoli, which was across from Barrington's Hospital, and we didn't know anyone there and had to pay the sixpence to go up in the gods. That was a harder picture house to sneak into as all the grown-ups went downstairs and we were sent up the stairs. I did sneak in there a few times, crawling up the stairs and waiting for the doorman to go to keep the noisy ones quiet, so I could sneak in. There was no lavatory upstairs, and some of the boys would pee on the floor, and it would drip onto the people below in the shilling seats, and there were always a few boys being kicked out for that.

On "bonfire night," when I got to the island, all the lads were sitting around a bonfire in the field and were talking about the time we had to have the gas masks fitted a few years ago.

Tommy was telling them about my running away from the Air Raid Precaution (ARP) at the Customs House on Rutland Street. "Tell us about it, Seanie," he said, as they all looked at me.

"It wasn't funny, Tommy," I said. "I could have died."

My mother had taken the three of us to have the gas masks fitted at the Air Raid Precaution yard, and when my turn came, the soldier took the rubber mask out of the little brown cardboard box that had a string on it to hang it around your neck. He put the straps around my head and told me to pull the mask around my face. I did, and it wasn't long before it was fogging up the goggles, and I couldn't breathe and I couldn't pull it off either. "It was stuck like an octopus to my face," I told the lads.

The soldier put his finger under the rubber and pulled it off, telling my mother he was sorry for forgetting to take the piece of cardboard out of the nozzle and she was looking at him with disbelief. So I grabbed the mask out of his hand and ran out the gate and down to the Shannon and threw it out into the outgoing tide. The lads all laughed about it.

"Well, tell them about the time when you and I were over at Bank Place when the farmer went into the pub, leaving his horse and cart full of piglets. Go on, Tommy. Tell 'em."

He started to laugh. "I'll tell 'em," he said, "and it was you, Seanie, who said pigs could fly."

"Well tell 'em what you done, then."

"Well, I got a straw out of the cart, and I told Seanie that I would show him pigs don't fly. I stuck the straw up one of the piglet's hole and blew into it. That's all."

"And tell them what happened," I said.

He hesitated, so I told the gang that the pig farted, and everyone was howling laughing except Tommy. He was glaring at me.

"That's why he couldn't fly, Tommy. You let the wind out," Christy said, holding his sides and roaring laughing.

"The piglet was squealing, and the farmer came out and chased us," Tommy said, still glaring at me.

"You would have got away with it if the pig hadn't squealed on you," said Pigeon, and the roaring laughing continued.

I didn't go to the Thomond that night after the bonfire, and I walked home to Robert Street feeling dejected at being so far from the island and the boys.

"There are no houses anywhere near our old butcher's shop and no kids to play with either," I told my mother as she wanted to know where I had been all day. I showed her the four pennies, and she said, "Is that all you made off the papers?"

I told her, "Everyone is selling the papers, and I was lucky to sell twenty-two at all."

One Saturday, I was working around the market, mostly carrying bundles of cabbage plants for the farmers. It was near planting time, and by the end of the day, I had eighteen shillings in my pants pocket. I was very proud to hand the money to my mother, and she had a big smile on her face.

One Monday afternoon when we were living in the Island Field and I got home from Creagh Lane, I was in a lot of pain from a terrible beating I'd gotten from Baldy McGuire, the headmaster. I had just left Christy, and he was after telling me that while I was out of class, Ned Kavanagh, our teacher, had thrown the wooden duster at Whacker. Whacker ducked, and the duster hit Christy right between the eyes, and that's why he had a big lump on his forehead.

I told him to pull my ganzey up and tell me what my back looked like. "It's lumpy to my touch," I told him, "and it hurts from the hiding from Baldy."

I had passed out as Baldy beat me with the leg off a chair up in his classroom, and when I woke up, the boys all stared at me as I walked past them and went down the iron staircase outside. "Seanie, you look like a giraffe. Your back is all red stripes. Don't let your mother see them, or she will find out you have been mooching again."

"She won't find out," I said, "and it's a zebra, not a giraffe that has stripes, Tarzan Christy."

Our mother came home from the Glenworth Hotel, and she had a shopping bag and fish and chips for our supper. She opened the bag and took out a pair of new black boots. "There now," she said to me, "put them on your feet and tell me if they fit you all right.

"They fit me all right, Mama," I said and walked around the room in my sockless boots, keeping a straight face while my backside and back seemed to be on fire. There was the strange feeling of having my feet confined, and the smell of the new leather filled my nostrils.

"Now you will be the talk of Creagh Lane," she said as she put the fish and chips out on the table and gave Frances hers on the bed. "Sit down now and have your suppers."

Breeda, Rosaleen, and Michael sat down, and I stood at the table.

"Sit down, Seanie," she said, laughing, "or you will wear out the new boots."

"I want to stand, Mama," I said, but she insisted that I sit at the table.

As I tried to obey, she saw that I was having difficulty sitting down and asked me what was the matter.

"Nothing Mama, it must be from carrying all the plants on Saturday at the market."

She came over to me and pulled my ganzey up. I could hear the breath almost leave her as she followed the stripes down, gently pulling my pants down behind.

"Who in the name of the suffering Jasus did this to you?" she wanted to know.

I hesitated as the others came around the table to have a look, seeing disbelief in their eyes. Breeda was saying, "Plants do that?"

My mother still had the knife in her hand she'd used to cut the loaf of bread. She wanted to know who had done this to me. I broke down and cried, telling her it was Baldy. I was waiting to hear her ask why but she didn't, and she went out the door to return with liniment from the chemist shop. She covered my back and backside with it before we went to bed, where I lay face down all night.

The following day, she put her old coat on, telling the others to stay in until she got home and to not answer the door to anyone. She took me by the hand and we walked down to Gerald Griffin School. I was having trouble walking and the ganzey was rubbing across my sore back as we went up the iron staircase in the yard, stopping at Baldy's classroom, my mother still holding my hand. She turned my back to the door and knocked. As the door opened, she lifted up my ganzey. "Did you do this to my son?" she asked him.

"And why are…" were the only words he got out as the broken glass showered me. My mother had brought a big milk bottle in her coat pocket and she'd struck him over his big bald head as he was leaning down to glare at me.

She took me by the hand and we walked down the stairs and out the door of the yard without a word being spoken. I was in a daze and could only stare at my mother in wonder as I hurried with her onto Bridge Street.

The boots were in my hand now as we walked down Bridge Street and across Mathew Bridge. Guard White cycled past, waving his finger at me. My mother asked, "What is that all about?"

"What, Mama?" I said.

"The guard waving his finger at you?"

"He does that to all the boys, Mama, and he doesn't like the boys from Creagh Lane."

The boots were in Pashy's the next day.

I was thinking it was a good job Guard White hadn't stopped to tell her about what I'd done the other day as I mooched. I had been coming home from Corkenree and had stopped to look through the crack in the door of the dead house at Barrington's, to see if there were any dead bodies on the slab. There was a body, but his head was off and lying sideways, looking at me. I stepped back in surprise because that was the first time I'd seen a head off a body.

Out of the corner of my eye, I caught a glimpse of Guard White coming straight for me on his sit-up-and-beg bike. I started to run but changed my mind and turned and ran toward him, to his surprise. As I passed him, he reached out to grab me by the hair. I ducked and could hear the bike's tires screeching as he braked on the wet road, the bike shuddering. I was gone before he could turn around and chase me over Baal's Bridge and up Irishtown.

Passing Riley's flour and pollard shop, I remembered Uncle Willy telling me about my father working for them. He said they must have been IRA themselves. My father drove the donkey and cart, delivering the pollard to the Grombana Creamery. He'd said a few times that the Black and Tans had stopped him but did not check him and the barrels of pollard with the guns, and they'd sent him on his way past the checkpoints. When he got through, the IRA were waiting for him farther up the road and took the guns out. Then he continued to the creamery. Uncle Willy said my father was eleven years of age then, and the Rileys were very good to him. The Black and Tans were searching all the houses and shops and most of the time stealing stuff as well. I wondered if Guard White had chased my father too like he chases me for mooching. My mother said that the Black and Tans gave her a box of biscuits after they broke a shop window up Dominic Street when she was small. She didn't mind them, she said, as long as they gave the kids the sweets and biscuits.

Uncle Willy said that my father had run away with Eamonn Mulcahy and Paddy Callopy a few years later and stowed away on a coal boat at the docks on its way to England. They were found on the boat and brought back to the docks. It seemed everyone wanted to go to England to find work.

Soon after this, our Aunt Nora and Uncle Mikey took us to their house in the Island Field as Aunt Nora said our mother was going away for a little bit and we would be all right there until she got back. I was not allowed to go back to Creagh Lane School since my mother had hit Baldy over the head.

We were never told where our mother had gone until I overheard Aunt Nora talking to Aunt Kitty. I was getting out of hand, she said, and she would be more than happy when Rosie got out of jail and put me in another school.

I decided to run away again and went to see Tommy to know if he wanted to run away with me to England. Tommy walked up William Street with me and he said he would think about it. "But we need money," he said.

We stopped outside the Munster and Leinster Bank on William Street and watched people going in and out. Then we followed one woman, staying close behind her as she went to the counter putting her purse on it. Tommy tapped her on one side and as she turned to see what he wanted, I grabbed the purse off the counter and ran out the door followed by Tommy. We ran down past Pachy Brown's pawn shop only stopping to grab a cake out of a bread and bun van delivering to one of the shops.

We stopped over at the Island bank, opened the purse and found ten pound note inside and nothing else. We decided it was a lot of money and we would hide it with the purse in the ground near a tree and wait for a few days to come back.

As I continued to go begging and stealing, I was excited, thinking about running away to England and not being chased by Guard White anymore and being back with the boys in the Island again. But during the day, I was on my own. Sometimes I would sit over on the Island bank but kept away from where we'd hidden the money near the baths.

About a week later, when nobody seemed to know about the bank robbery, I went to tell Tommy that we should go get the money now. We went to the hiding place and found that it was gone.

I looked at Tommy with suspicion and he was looking at me. "I didn't tell anyone where it was. Did you?" I said, as he looked away.

"Only my sister," he said, "but I didn't tell where it was hidden."

"Well, we won't be going to fecking England after all," I told him as I walked away dejected with the seed of mistrust planted.

We were all excited when our mother came home to Aunt Nora's and we all went back to 10 Robert Street. My mother said it was time for me to go back to school and one morning took me up to Sexton Street Christian Brothers' School. She knocked at the door. A Christian brother came out and she asked him if they would take me. He asked her why I was coming there, and she told him that I'd been badly beaten at Creagh Lane and she didn't want me there anymore. He never asked why I was beaten, he just said they were full up and there was no room, and he closed the door in our faces. I couldn't get into a Christian Brothers' school anywhere in Limerick and I wasn't unhappy with that. I wasn't educated but I could work or steal and beg if that's what it took, I thought.

One day, my mother came home from town, and she said there was a school that would take me in. "What school, Mama?" I asked.

"Leamy's," she said.

It was drizzling rain as I walked around aimlessly up in the Irishtown. I was thinking about having to go to a school that the boys said was full of mostly snobby rich kids, and I would have to wear shoes and stockings all the time there. "It's not like Creagh Lane and there's no one there from the Island either. I heard that some rich Americans went there as well," Dano Kelly told me. "Maybe they know your rich cousins in America. You will have to make them give you some of their sandwiches. Bunny Wells will be wondering where you went to and have more of his sandwiches for himself," he said laughing.

"I didn't take half of his sandwiches anymore," I said. "He's my friend now and he has no father either. His mother makes him wear those nice clothes and shoes and stockings, he told me."

There were all kinds of thoughts racing through my mind as I slowly made my way down the Irishtown, making my way past Barrington's Hospital where I bumped into Tommy. "Where are you going?" I asked.

"Back to the fecking class and I'm taking the long way back. I'm fecking fed up of school. "You're lucky you got away from Baldy, I am almost being killed because of him," he said.

"Why?" I asked.

"He sent me down the Island to Mousy's house at bun and milk time to see if Mousy was coming to school. I knocked on the door and his mother answered. I asked her if Mousy was coming to school. She said, 'Come in love,' and she nearly beat the daylights out of me. I thought she had gone mad and she said that she doesn't want us to ever to call him Mousy again. If it wasn't for me sister passing and putting a stop to it, I would have been dead. Timmy's mother or Jimmy's mother doesn't do that to us, Seanie. I'm going to tell Mousy to tell me his real name or I will never go to his house again. What are you going to do, Seanie?"

"Don't know, but I will tell you one thing, I won't be going to no fecking school called Leamy's. I'll run away first."

"Did you know Scooba got a kick in the forehead from the folly horse?" he asked.

"No I did not," said I.

"Well, he is up in St. John's Hospital and his forehead has the horse shoe stamped on it!"

"Oh poor Scooba, I am sorry for him. That fecking horse is a terror, Tommy. I will go and see him."

"The horse, Seanie?" he cracked.

"No, you fecking idgit."

Tommy made his way, laughing, back to school to tell Baldy that Mousy was sick and couldn't come to school today.

I went toward the potato market and up Bridge Street, passing Creagh Lane. I could hear the class reading out loud, almost singing, through an open window opposite the bust of Gerald Griffin. I paused and smiled to myself remembering throwing the stick from the bottom of the big map of Ireland, spear-like, out the open window and into the Protestant graveyard of St. Mary's across the road when Brother Cody was out of the classroom. A cheer had gone up from the boys. "He will not have that weapon to beat us with no more," I said with a grin. He would have killed me if he'd found out.

I continued to stroll, still smiling, as I reached Nicholas Street. The bells of the Catholic Church of St. Mary's farther down started to ring. I thought it was the Angelus, but it was too early. Something else, I thought, as I stopped and blessed myself.

No Guard White, I hoped, as I made my way towards Barrington's Hospital after I turned into Mary Street, passing the Garda station with a little more pace in my gait. I once again peeped through the crack in the doors to see if there was a body on the slabs—not today, and I turned the corner in front of the hospital.

I looked across at the railings in front of the hospital and saw an old bike leaning there. It was a man's bike and I thought I would take it for a spin. I hadn't been on a bike before but it looked easy. I took the bike and the first thing I found was that I couldn't sit on the saddle and had to put my legs between the cross bar. After falling over a few times, I was getting better staying up with only a few scratches and bumps to show for it. I was enjoying the riding around the street and cycled farther and farther away. Now I was riding around the potato market's cobbled yard, memories of the bikes our father had promised us and the thought of having to go to a new school were bothering me. I turned the bike and started riding across Matthew Bridge around Bank Place. No sign of Bunny, but I didn't expect to see him as he never missed school. I carried on cycling up Patrick Street past Arthur's Quay where the limping Mikey Raleigh's boys played in a band. They were marching around the streets playing with their tin whistles and drums. Then into O'Connell Street, passing the horse and carts and a few motor cars. Somehow, I found myself on the Dock Road and continued past Corkenree. I could feel the cool breeze off the Shannon through the hole in the backside of my short pants. It was exciting as this was the farthest I had ever gone on the Dock Road. It was all new scenery to me as I went past the point of no return, making my mind up to keep going away from the confusion and anger I felt. Kicked out of our house, kicked out of school, I would run away for good. I cycled past towns I had only heard of but especially Foynes, remembering Mary, the cat, and my mother's laugh as she told everyone on St. Ita's Street about the story. Her laugh was a rare occurrence now.

The rain was teeming down all day and the evening light was fading as I peddled into the approach of a village and saw the sign on the road: "An Gleann." This caused me to stop peddling and slowly pull off the road and into the grassy side. I was drenched to the skin and very hungry. Coming toward me there was a lad sitting on his donkey, which was pulling a cart. I waited until he was close to me. He was younger than myself, I could see, and I waved to him. He pulled the reins on the donkey and gave me an odd look as I asked him what the English name for the village was.

"Where are you from?" he wanted to know.

"I'm from Limerick," I said proudly to him.

"How did you get all the way here?" he then asked.

"On me bike," I said.

He looked at the bike and then at me. "It's a big bike," said he.

"It's me father's," I told him. I didn't realize at the time I was telling him the truth.

"This is Glin," he continued.

THE OLD BARRINGTONS BIKE
Seanie Morrison

Thirty two miles or much more had I rode
through hail and the sleet and cold wind alike
counting each marker upon the grey road
running away on the old Barringtons bike.

Riding through Foynes and eight miles further on
the night closing on me and no carbide to light
I happened upon a small town called "An Gleann"
when the terror did grip me I neer died of the fright.

For had she not told me time time and again
my stealing and mooching would break her poor heart
my time running out a step nearer to Glin
they would haul me away on a horse and a cart.

I peddled like mad my leg tween the cross bar
my heart racing wildly and my mind full alert
the pain from the hunger now near and then far
my capture was swift in the town of Tarbert.

I don't know if he saw my face turn white and my famished body shake as I pushed off even with my aching legs and feet sore from the peddles. I left him sitting on his donkey watching me disappear down the road. I glanced back, peddling like mad, trying to distance myself from what was the most feared name to the boys of Limerick. *Glin.*

"And may God help you," everyone always said.

"The Christian Brothers have cat-o-nine-tails and whip you for the least thing," Christy said to me one day. "And they starve you too. They make you work all day and even at night."

"How do you know that, Christy?" I asked.

"Well a lad escaped, and my mother said it was in the Limerick papers all about it. She told me what happens if you are sent there," he said.

I believed him and I believed my mother and Guard White and even Baldy as I sped out of "An Gleann," its Gaelic name, and kept going away from Limerick and the dreaded Glin where the boys' prison, St. Joseph's Industrial School, was said to be.

Three miles on and I came to another small town. I was completely exhausted now and my stomach was aching from the hunger. I saw the name "Tarbert" on the sign on the road and wondered if that was Gaelic as well, but I didn't ask anyone. The only thing on my mind was food, any food, as I placed the bike against the wall of a shop and looked in the big window. The shop was dark and closed. I walked around the town, but all the shops were closed. I came to where there was a lit sign in blue over the door, and it said "Garda" on the three sides. In desperation, I decided to go in and give myself up. I hoped that they would take me back to Limerick where I could get something to eat at home.

I went up the three steps and the door was open as I pushed on it and went in. There was a look of surprise on the big, rosy-cheeked policeman's face. He reminded me of the pictures I've seen of Santa Claus. He asked me what I wanted and I said that I wanted to go home to Limerick and that I was hungry. He wanted to know how I had come thirty-five miles from Limerick. I told him I'd borrowed the bike and got lost in the dark. He asked me where my bike was and I told him as he led me to get it from outside the shop. He remarked that it was a little big for me.

"I put my leg inside the crossbar," I said, showing him the oil from the chain on my calf.

"Who loaned you the bike?" he wanted to know.

"It's me father's," I told him as we walked back to the garda station.

"Does your father know you borrowed his bike?" he asked.

"He doesn't," said I.

"That's like stealing," he reminded me as we went back inside the station.

"Me father is in England, and he told me that I could borrow the bike until he comes home," I lied, getting nervous of all the questioning.

"You will stay here tonight, and we will take you back home tomorrow," he said as he led me into a cell where he said I would sleep until the morning. He came back with a mug of steaming hot tea and a sandwich, of what, I didn't know, nor did I care as I shoved it hungrily into my eager mouth. He told me to use the little towel he gave me to dry myself off and to give him my clothes to hang in front of the fire. I gave him my soaking ganzey but wouldn't take off my wet short pants, which would have left me naked. "Well, dry your pants with the towel," he ordered me, when he saw I wouldn't take them off.

I lay down on the hard wooden bench in the cell and that's all I remembered until being woken in the morning by a strange face. "What's your name," he asked.

"Seanie Morrisey," I replied.

"And what are you doing here in Tarbert, Seanie?" he asked.

"I was out riding me bike and got lost," said I.

"And where in Limerick do you live?" he wanted to know.

I paused and thought that I better not say 10 Robert Street, the abandoned butcher shop where we were living, as we would be evicted as our mother had said. So I lied and told him I lived at 121 St. Munchin's Street in Island field; Aunt Nora's house.

I was taken to the car where I saw the front wheel of the bike sticking out of the boot in the back of the car. There I was handed two slices of brown bread with thick slices of bacon between, by the rosy-cheeked garda who said, "Good luck now." I didn't know if he was saying that to me or to the garda driving the car as we pulled away from the curve.

It wasn't long before we were going past the town of Glin along the road by the Shannon River. The only view I had was the hill going up through the town on the right with little shops and terraced houses, and then it was gone. I wondered where the prison of St. Joseph's was but dared not to ask. I was thankful that we had passed the place altogether.

About an hour later, we arrived at Mary Street Garda Station. I was led inside, followed by the bike, which the garda put inside. I was told to sit at the table in the office and sometime later, a garda came in. He asked me where I had gotten the bike, as Father Lee had reported to them that his bike was missing from outside Barrington's Hospital where he had gone to give the Last Rites to a man who was dying.

I felt ashamed and kept my eyes down. I was looking at the floor as I confessed that I had borrowed the old bike just to learn to ride it. I would have brought it back except I rode it too far away.

The garda went to Aunt Nora's and brought her up to Mary Street to me. She told them that my mother was at work and that she would look after me until my mother got home to her house where she stayed while waiting for another council house to be allotted to her. He told Aunt Nora that I had stolen the priest's bike and there was a record of my mooching from school before being expelled from Creagh Lane. He mentioned the assault by my mother on a helpless headmaster, Brother McGuire, who had several stitches put in a gash on his head and he wanted to know which school I was attending at present.

Aunt Nora told him she knew all about Brother McGuire. She told him that she had seen what the six-foot brother had done to a helpless child with her own eyes. "If she had her way," she said, "she would have added a few more stitches." As for my stealing the bike, she said she would talk to my mother and she would punish me herself with her own hand.

"His mother is waiting to hear from the Office of National Education to see which school he will be taken by, and as it was near Christmas, the offices were closed."

"I didn't steal the bike, Aunt Nora," I interrupted. "I only borrowed it."

"Will you whisht, Seanie!" she said back as she asked the garda, "Would that be all now, sir?"

"I'm going to issue a summons for him to appear before a judge on February 5, 1949, and we're expecting either you or his guardian to represent him at the court on that day and hour," he told her. He handed her the docket saying that the school's guard, White, was sick and tired of chasing me all around Limerick, and Aunt Nora took me by the hand and out the door.

"Seanie Morrissey, you will have your poor mother in the mental home if you don't stop this carrying on," Aunt Nora chastised me as we stopped at the top of Bridge Street. Hearing the Angelus ring out from Saint Mary's, we blessed ourselves after a minute of silence in prayer. "I don't know what you will tell Father Lee at confession on Saturday," she went on. "Why in the name of the loving Jasus did you take his bike and he doing God's work at the hospital?"

"I didn't know it was his bike, Aunt Nora," I said sheepishly.

"If your mother had the few pounds to get your cursed bike that your good-for-nothing father sent over from England, none of this would have happened. Instead it's in front of a judge again, she is, and God only knows how much that will cost her."

"It was Breeda's bike, Aunt Nora," I reminded her with an inquisitive tone, but she didn't respond, which left me thinking of what she had said.

It was two days before my mother would let me out of the house on Robert Street and only then for me to go with her boyfriend Joe out the Dublin Road to a small farm where he said his cousin lived and where we could dig up some spuds and cabbage. I took the journey back to Robert Street back down the Dublin Road with the bag of potatoes and cabbage on my back, my legs bandy from the weight. Joe walked ahead of me with a Woodbine cigarette hanging from his mouth, glancing back at me and telling me, "Not far to go now," as we passed some gypsies at the cooperage, shaking their heads as I stumbled.

"What you got in the bag?" one shouted.

Joe shouted back, pulling the fag out of his mouth, "Mind your own fucken business," as he pulled me along by the shoulder of my ganzey, but didn't make an effort to relieve me of the heavy bag.

The gypsies threatened to take the bag off me, but they were too drunk and staggering all around the road.

Where we squatted, bunting strung from the roof.

As we approached the Irishtown, it began drizzling rain again. We continued to pass black-shawled women and flat-capped men, a familiar sight all over Limerick. We stopped across the road by the market, Joe telling me, "Seanie, wait here a minute till I see if the road is clear. We should not be seen entering number 10 Robert Street."

We carefully slipped inside into the darkness as the grey blanket was up on the big shop window. My mother lit the candle on the chair and looked at all the potatoes and heads of cabbage in the coal bag. "Lovely," she said. "Now, our Kitty over in Ballynanty will boil up a few for us when we go over. There is enough for all of us. All we need now is a pig's head. Does your sister have any pigs out at the farm, Joe?" she said laughing.

Christmas came and went and my memory is of the stockings hanging over the fireplace with the usual apple, orange, and a few nuts; our presents, which we were thrilled with. The one Christmas, our father came over from England with a die cast with which he made lead soldiers for me. I later chewed their heads off after playing with them, so he made no more. Just memories now as I walked with Joe with our hand-lines to go fishing for bream in the Abbey River across from the cooperage.

We came home with a couple of nice bream and big grins across our faces, handing them to my mother, with the girls and Michael google-eyed at the still-live fish. Our mother cooked them and sat for dinner, smiling and saying, "There are more bones in these bream than are up Mount St. Lawrence graveyard." She picked the little bones out of her mouth. It's a wonder we're all still living "What with the old rubber chickens they gave Seanie for payment at that chicken place and fish that would choke the very life out of you."

"Rosie, you would be eating pheasant and salmon if there was any work to be had in Limerick," Joe said as he put on his trilby hat and walked out into the darkness of the damp night. Where to, we didn't know and we never asked. He was just a friend, our mother had told us.

Sitting on the wall outside the Tivoli Cinema as the Abbey River raced high below me, I was unable to get in to see the *King Kong* movie that was on that week after being on at the Lyric earlier.

There was a commotion at Baals Bridge and everyone was running there to see what was going on. One of the Guinness horse-drawn barges loaded with small barrels of Guinness had broken loose, and crashed into the bridge. I watched as the barrels disappeared off the deck as fast as the tide was running. Men were passing barrel after barrel up to eager waiting hands as the man on the bank on the far side of the river watched helplessly, holding the reins of his horse. "He has had his eleven pints, I bet," I heard Mr. Tobin, one of the men saying, waving to him as he walked away with a barrel on his shoulder.

As he walked away, one of my friends, John Fahy, told me that he lived near Mr. Tobin. He told me he had eighteen children and would be drunk for a month now.

Aunt Nora was sick when we went down to the Island Field to see if the woman who had moved into our house had anymore letters that had been sent to 76 St. Ita's Street and been given to her. There were none, so as Aunt Nora lay on her bed upstairs, Mama said she would read the old letter again that she had in her pocket

"I still haven't heard from Mary or Peggy or anyone," Aunt Nora said, "and it is going on for years, not one word after all these years."

Mama sat on the corner of the bed with an opened letter saying that the fleas were hopping mad around her already.

"Gesh out with you Rosie Plunkett, tis you who brought them with you from Robert Street. Go on with you now and read the letter."

240 Lucille Ave.

Elmont, Long Island

Sept. 8, 1945

Dear Rosie,

Thought I would drop you a few lines. I feel a little blue today. I went up to see Jack's grave. It looked very lonely there. My Kitty left for nurse training Monday. She's been gone three and a half years. My heart is very lonely. Now I know how my poor mother felt when we left her. It's funny you don't realize these things until you are too old. I haven't seen Tommy since they went back home last week. They didn't even drop a line. He is probably working hard to get enough money to buy a house out by Peg. She lives away out the island. I live more near New York City. Don't say anything about it if you are writing to them. I am sending a little package today. They don't accept over four pounds at the post office, and only once a month they let you send anything out of the country. Maybe now that the war is over, they may change that. I hope so. Anyway, how are things with you? Will you ask Nora and Kitty if you can send me their address so I can write to them? Nora doesn't know me, but I remember her as a little baby. That said, how are they making out? How are their families? How is Paddy and family? Tommy said something about bringing him out here, but as I said, he will have to take the whole family as they would probably be heartbroken if he just took Paddy. Tommy misses Jack terribly because they used to call each other on the phone every night. Jack was feeling good when he left the house. Joe, his wife, said he got an attack of indigestion and died from that, but the people he worked with said it was a heart attack he died of because he complained of a pain in his heart the night before, and his wife didn't realize he should have seen the doctor. She's going home to her mother now and taking the two children. Jack's eldest daughter has red hair, just like our sister Kitty. She has a face like Jack when he was her age, but the boy looks like his mother, Joe Glawins. Jack worked seven days a week, so he had plenty of money to send home to Joe Glawins' mother. Now he is gone, and Joe is going home. Jack hasn't been very happy for quite a few years but don't say anything to anyone what I tell you, Rose, so I will finish now because I may say too much, so with lots of love from myself and family to your little family, I close.

Write soon if you can.

Sister Mary.

"Now, Rosie, will you tell me this one thing? Why in the name of the mother of Jasus, why I haven't had one word from any of them over in America in all these years?" Aunt Nora wanted to know. "I know you sent my address, so what is happening?"

"That Nora, I could not tell you, but they said that the Germans were sinking all of the ships in the Atlantic Ocean, and maybe that's why neither yourself, me neither, nor Kitty have heard anything for such a long time."

"Rosie, the war is over three long years. Will you write and ask Mary if her inkwell run dry, and tell her to drop me-self a line before the tide goes out in Island Field?"

My mother promised she would as we went out the front door.

"I don't know where Mary's letters would be sent to at all, and if she sent a couple of dollars in them, we would never know. Sure, I couldn't bring meself to tell her that Sonny Morrison has not come back from England, and we were evicted out of the house at 76. I would be ashamed of meself, Kitty," our mother was telling Aunt

Kitty as we sat over at her house in Ballananty Beg, having a cup of tea.

"I have been living a lie all this time with not telling them, not since our Paddy died and poor Kathleen having the children taken away from her by the court. Have I written to Mary or any of them in America? Will you look at the cutting from the newspaper that I kept, which I don't think yourself or Nora saw as you never mentioned anything, and I didn't want to upset anyone either with all the troubles we have ourselves. We all broke our hearts as it was and 'tis only now that I should show you it, Kitty. We all knew what happened to the children and poor Kathleen finishing up in the mental hospital at St. Joseph's, but no one mentioned it being in the papers. And who can afford to buy the papers, anyway? There's enough gossip going for free without looking in the papers, but go on and read what the papers said, anyway. She will never be let out of that place, Kitty."

My mother took the cutting out of her bag and handed it to Aunt Kitty, but she handed it back saying, "You read it, Rosie. My eyes are not as good as they used to be.

"Between yourself and Nora, ye are all going blind," she replied as she started to read the cutting to Kitty. She must have forgotten me sitting by the front door, watching the others playing in the street with our cousins Rita and Mary. She said the headline was *Mother Frightened – Left Children Unattended"* and went on.

> *A mother of three children, Mrs. Kathleen Plunkett, of 13 Nicholas Street was prosecuted by the NSPCC, said the city court yesterday, for neglecting her three children.*
>
> *Inspector Foley, NSPCC, said that he found the three children fully dressed, sleeping in a narrow bed in an upstairs room. There was a lighted candle on a chair near a box of matches. Several burn marks of candles were plainly visible on other chairs. One child's leg sticking out from under the bed clothes*

was within inches of the candle. There was a great danger of fire. The living conditions were very bad. He interviewed the mother, whose husband was dead. She usually left the house at 6:00 p.m. and returned at all hours of the morning. She sometimes slept with her mother, three-quarters of a mile away. The defendant said she was frightened to sleep in the house. She got up one morning and found the door opened.

JUSTICE: And you leave the children to sleep by themselves?

DEFENDANT: I only left them one night.

INSPECTOR: She stays in during the day.

Justice's Remarks

JUSTICE: I have sympathy with you because you lost your husband. But you should mind your children and keep them clean. The court can send you to jail, and you really deserve to go there. You have risked the children's lives by bringing them up in this fashion.

MR. CALEB MACUTCHEON, SOIR FOR THE NSPCC: These children are living under appalling conditions and they have no chance at all.

Defendant's Undertaking

JUSTICE: I will adjourn this case for fourteen days for a report from the probation officer if the defendant gives an undertaking to stay with her children. I will then decide whether to send them away or not.

The defendant gave the undertaking, and the case was adjourned for fourteen days.

"If the TB hadn't taken poor Paddy, none of this would be happening. 'Tis a curse, Rosie. What I don't like about the room above

Marcella's chip shop is there's no lavatory and little Noreen passing me one morning as I went up the stairs to see Kathleen and give her a can of sour milk for her to make the bread and she, the little thing, struggling to come down with the bucket to empty on the street, the bucket spilling all the way down. At least we have a lavatory here in these new corporation houses, Rosie."

"Talk for yourself, Kitty," my mother said, reminding her of our own bucket by the bed in Robert Street.

One day, our mother went to the General Post Office and informed them that we had a new address and asked them to please forward any letters to St. Munchin's Street in the future instead of 76 St. Ita's Street in St. Mary's Park.

"Do you mean Island Field?" the post master asked.

"I do, sir," my mother replied as she filled out the form.

"And to whom would I be forwarding the letters, missus?"

"To meself," our mother informed him.

"And who would be yourself?"

I looked at Breeda and started to laugh.

"Why are you laughing?" our mother inquired, glaring down on the both of us.

"He sounds like Gurky McMahon, Mama," I blurted out, and Breeda busted out laughing in the post office.

"Rosie Plunkett, I mean, Morrison," our mother corrected.

"Plunkett Morrison. Put that down on the form under the name section on the form."

"'Tis Morrison and not Plunkett Morrison," our mother said back to him, looking a little frustrated. "And you two are giving me a headache," she said, looking at the postmaster and telling him the children were getting harder to keep quiet, and she was getting confused with all the filling out forms lately. He said he understood and told us to wait outside until our mother finished filling out the form.

Walking back to Robert Street in the drizzling rain, our mother wanted to know what all the merriment had been about in the post office and what devilment had Gurky been up to this time in the Island Field to have us make a feck of her with all the laughing going on. Just then Rosaleen came toward us, pushing the pram full of straw for the mattress from Cantillion's. Much to my relief. I would have had to use the swearword, shithouse, and she would have killed me, so I didn't want to tell her what Jimmy's mother was after telling the other boys' mothers about what the latest was from Gurky and what his wife, Raleigh, had been telling Mary Cronin, Jimmy's mother, as everyone called her instead of Roche.

Jimmy had told us that he'd overheard Mrs. McMahon telling her that an official saying he was from the corporation had been asking Mrs. Donoghue, "How was the *latrine* working?" And sure, no one in Island Field would know what he was talking about, and he went on to ask her, "How's the *lavatory* working?" Another name she wasn't familiar with as she had only recently come out of the lanes like the rest of us and the bucket was all she knew. He got very annoyed at her as she kept saying "WHAT?"

He ranted at her, asking, "Was the shithouse working?" and she up and tells him that he was up in Halpin's pub having a pint, and he hadn't worked a day since he fell off the plank with a half hundred weight bag of coal on his back at the docks.

Time and memories seemed to race through my childhood as I became more and more rebellious at being controlled, especially in going to school, something I would regret later on in my life.

I would miss each and every one from the Island, including my family, when the day arrived for the walk to the courthouse and the hanging judge, Judge Gleeson. At thirteen years and seven months of age, my freedom roaming the streets was coming to an end.

It was February 5th, 1949, when I was sentenced and taken from the courthouse on Merchant's Quay, the only one of several other boys, I later learned. My mind flashed back to when I had cycled past the dreaded town, Glin, and a shiver ran down my spine as I glanced at my mother. As I was led out, I saw a tear run down her cheek as she forced a smile. *Keep the chin up,* she seemed to say as I saw her lips move, and then she shouted, "I will come and see you soon, Seanie!"

I wondered when. I was to be released when I reached the age of sixteen, which seemed an eternity. The judge said that I should be flogged for what I had done, and I wondered if they used the cat-o'-nine-tails, like they did on Gerard Fogarty last. (He said they stripped him naked, tied his wrists to the handrails leading up to Saint Patrick's dormitory, and flogged him until he passed out.) I recalled Baldy McGuire, but Gerard was out now, and I was on my way in.

After the short walk up Bridge Street past the school and into Mary Street Garda Station, I stood holding the bars of the cell, staring at the big, burly garda, who assured me that it would not be too bad in Glin. "You will have shoes on your feet and a coat on your back, and they will put some meat on those bones," he said. "You look very pale and tired."

I told him I was hungry, but he just shrugged his shoulders and left. *Not as nice as the garda in Tarbert,* I thought. There was silence in the cell except for the rumbling in my stomach, until I heard the familiar voice of the priest as he entered the holding cell area of the garda station. An ashen, stern-faced Father Lee was staring down on me through the bars, berating me for taking his old bike, which was a deadly sin, a mortal sin, he said. "Shame on you," he said. "What's your name?"

"Seanie, Father," I replied.

"Don't call me Father." His voice was rising. "I'm not your father. Where is your father?"

"He's in England, Fa..." I stopped. "He is over in England."

"He should be here, and I would give him a piece of my mind. I was giving the Last Rites in the hospital, and you stole my bike."

"I didn't steal it, Fa..." I stopped again. "I only took it for a spin."

"'A spin,' says you. Thirty-odd miles and meself having to walk all the way back to Saint Mary's. Well, you won't be taking a spin for a while now, will you? Say the rosary ten times, six Hail Marys, and an Our Father six times, and ask for God's forgiveness while you are on your way to the industrial school in Glin, and may God forgive you. That's all I have to say to you." At which he left, and I heard him thank the garda for the recovery of his old bike.

I was taken from the cell, the policeman having a firm grip on my wrist, and led to the car on Mary Street, where I was placed into the passenger seat next to the driver. I looked at my numb white hand and watched the blood flow back slowly as I twitched my fingers, looking across the road and seeing my Aunt Nora waving to me and crying openly. It made me very sad to see her crying. She was so thin, and her hair was hanging limp from the soaking, drizzling rain. I wondered where my mother was. She would be at Robert Street, I thought. Breeda was not well at all lately. She was waking us all up in the bed at night and coughing up blood in the bucket. She had been to the dispensary, but our mother never said what was up with her. Maybe it was something to do with her having Saint Vitus' dance, I thought and regretted having teased her about it all this time, calling her giddy biddy.

Imposing buildings of St. Joseph's Industrial School, Glin, Co. Limerick seen through an early morning Shannon Estuary haze in the winter of 1972   Photograph: Ray O'Donoghue

The car pulled away from the curb and turned left down Bridge Street, and I heard some screaming from the chemist shop at the corner and did not know who it was as we sped over Matthew Bridge past Blank Place. I saw Bunny Wells sitting on the steps of the tenement where he lived. He would have his buns to himself now, I thought.

There were no other cars on the road as we wound our way on the lonely road, seeing a horse and a cart now and again, watching the stone mile-markers with the miles to go carved into the stone every mile, leaving the hustle and bustle of the city behind, with only the noise of the engine interrupting my thoughts—thoughts of the family squatting in the abandoned butcher shop: *Who will go out begging on the Ennis Road now? Michael is too small and Breeda too delicate and I've never seen girls out begging anyway.* I wondered how they would survive at all. *Jasus, I'll be a man before I get out.* Correcting my taking the Lord's name in vain, I said, "Sorry, God," getting a sideways glance from the driver.

Glin, Co. Limerick.

It was making me nervous. The farther we left Limerick behind and the nearer we got to Glin, not a word was spoken, and my thoughts raced back and forth, with visions of being tied to the rails and being flogged with the cat-o'-nine-tails, beatings, beatings, beatings. I was sick and tired of the beatings. I remembered Christy saying that my back looked like I was a giraffe, and I smiled to myself. He didn't know a giraffe from a zebra even after watching all the *Tarzan* pictures at the Thomond picture house. My smile quickly left as I watched the town of Foynes disappear in the rear-view mirror.

The driver interrupted my thoughts. "Not too far from Glin now."

"I know," I replied.

He did not question that knowledge and continued staring out the front window of the car as if in a trance, his legs moving up and then down on the pedals on the floor, and he was moving a lever in the middle every now and then. My Uncle Johnny used to do that, driving the rubbish corporation lorry when he used to give me a ride when I was very small. I would have plenty of time to remember all the great times in Limerick, I thought, plenty of time, almost three years.

Suddenly the sign *An gleann* seemed to jump out of the ground as if the devil himself had pushed it out of the hobs of Hell. A cold wind blowing off the Shannon River added to the shiver running down my spine. Turning left off the road, the car labored going up the hill as I watched the little shops slowly pass by; Culhanes Drapers and others as we wound up the hill and entered Saint Joseph's. We stopped at the gate where the garda spoke with a man there, and we proceeded toward some depressing, two-story-high grey-stone buildings. A wall surrounded us, and I thought that I could easily climb over that. Gus Hanley's orchard wall was higher. I didn't see any broken glass bottles cemented onto the top either, like Gus had (and the scars on my knees and hands bore witness to). We passed one block, and I counted nine windows, then a door and another three windows, then iron gates, before stopping after another six windows at the big doors. I don't know why I was counting windows and doors. Maybe it was to distract my thoughts of what might happen when we stopped at the second building.

There was a Christian brother standing by the door as if waiting for me; a stern-faced, robed brother greeting the garda who was closest to him through the open window of the car. The garda got out and shook his hand as if they were old friends and was telling me to get out as he came around and opened the door. I stood at the side of the car, terrified at the thought of what would happen next. They spoke softly at length, the brother looking past the garda at me a couple of times, and I was wondering what the garda was telling him. I finally heard the brother telling the garda in a raised voice to come inside and he would get Mary to bring a cup of tea. I would later learn that there were two women at the school; the brothers' cook and a nurse for the boys and the brothers.

The garda went in, and I began to follow for my cup of tea. As I passed the brother, he caught me by the ear, and he almost lifted me off the ground. "Steal a priest's bike, would you?" he hissed through clenched teeth. "You come with me," he said, as if I had an alternative, still holding me by my throbbing ear. He hauled me through the steel gates past a chapel on a path leading to another grey building farther back from the front ones. *Deeper into Hell,* I thought, my ear burning and very painful.

This was my introduction to Glin by Brother Breen, as the boys would later tell me, and he was one of the better brothers, they said.

We stopped at an open door, another brother came out, and Brother Breen addressed him. "Brother Cullen, this one stole the priest's bike. He is a thief," and at that, he walked away.

Brother Cullen told me to enter the store. I learned later that he was in charge of all supplies coming into the school – bedding, cloth for the tailor's shop, leather for the shoemaker's shop, springs for the bedspring shop, and food for the brothers and the over two hundred "inmates," a name I likened to myself and the others who had been sent in for stealing, and not the other poor, misfortunate boys who, through no fault of their own, had been sentenced to suffer the same indignities as ourselves. I was to kindle lifelong friendships and associations to suffer with many inmates and orphans. Sadly, some could not cope and chose to end the memories after their release while others distanced themselves from society.

"Sit there," Brother Cullen ordered me, sizing me up and looking at my bare feet. "When last did you wash your feet?" he wanted to know.

"Last week."

"Last week what?"

"Last Friday."

"Last Friday what?"

I was puzzled and just looked at him, wondering what he was talking about.

"Whilst you are here in Saint Joseph's, you will address all the brothers as sir. Now when did you last wash your feet?"

I hesitated and replied, "Last week, sir."

"That's better. There's a tap outside the door. Go and wash your feet now."

As he followed me outside, I washed my feet and followed him back into the storeroom.

"Sit," he instructed me, handing me a pair of socks and asking what size of boots I took.

"Don't know."

"Don't know what?"

"Oh, don't know, sir."

As I put the socks on my feet, he came with a pair of leather boots. "Here, try these on."

I tried on the boots and got up to walk a short distance but found it difficult, and he asked, "Do they fit?"

"They are awful tight, sir." I was getting the hang of the *sir* bit now, I thought. There were nails sticking inside the boots. They were bent down, so they did not stick in my feet, but they got caught in the socks as I pulled the boots off again. "Do I have to wear boots, sir? They hurt my feet."

"As long as you are here in Saint Joseph's you will wear boots. Now try these," he said, handing me a bigger-size pair of boots. They slipped on easily, and I again walked the short distance without complaining. He had seen that they were too big, like boats, I thought. But, before I could tell him, he quipped, "You will grow into them. When did you last have a shower?"

"About two days ago, sir." I thought we were becoming friendly.

"Well, why did you tell me you washed your feet a week ago?"

I'd thought he was talking about the weather in Limerick as I had never had a shower like he was talking about. "I had a bath, sir," I corrected after remembering hearing about showers when he asked again when I washed my feet.

A grin crossed his face as he turned away from me. "Well, you are just in time for a shower. Here in Saint Joseph's, the boys have showers every other week on this day, and I will give you these pants and jumper to put on, after you have your shower."

When the boys came out from their classes, he then handed me a small towel and a piece of red carbolic soap. "Follow me," he said, leaving the store and locking it. He pointed at the iron-railed stairs and beckoned me to go up ahead of him. I couldn't help thinking of Gerard Fogarty, Gerard's dormitory, and the very same stairs they tied him to. *Oh sweet Jesus—the flogging stairs—don't let them do that to me,* I thought as I climbed the stairs, stopping at the opening into the dormitory.

"Go on," he said as I hesitated. "Take off your boots."

I stepped out of the new boots, again freeing the socks off the bent nails, and looking at the rows of small, neatly made beds. And, after he pushed me forward, I walked in, looking back at him every now and again as we walked all the way to the end of the dormitory, where there was another doorway that was a washroom. "This is your bed," he rasped. "This is the washroom. You will wait here until I come back for you. Sit on the bed. Whilst here in Saint Joseph's," he informed me, "you will kneel at it each night and say your prayers before going to sleep. The night watchman will be keeping his eye on you in case you get the notion to leave the dormitory during the night. You will get up each morning at half-past five, wash your face, and will follow the other boys to the chapel for six o'clock Mass. After Mass, you will come back here with the other boys and make your bed exactly as you see it made. Now that's if you haven't soiled the bed before going to the dining hall for breakfast, where I will be before assigning you to a classroom. If you soil or wet the bed, you will stay here until I come up, and I will punish you severely. You will not have breakfast. Now, I will be back shortly." He walked past the rows and rows of little beds on the polished wooden floor and descended the dreaded whipping stairs out of sight.

Silence except for *drip-drip-drip* of the taps in the lavatory, as I sat waiting. I didn't know how long I sat there swinging my legs and looking at the new stockings every now and then. It had been a long time since the Saint Vincent De Paul Holy Communion socks rotted, I thought. First the boot soles wore off. My mother put cardboard in the boots to cover the holes, but the cardboard got wet anyway, and the socks were always wet, and they rotted, and I was back on my feet again.

I lay back on the bed. I was very tired. The next thing I knew, I was wakened with a terrible pain across my legs. I jumped up and saw Brother Cullen standing there with the raised, well-recognized leather over his shoulder, striking me again and again all over my body and calling me a thief, a sinner, and worthless, as I cringed on my knees by the side of the bed. "You will never again go to sleep during the day," he reminded me, putting the long, heavy leather back inside of his pocket of his frock. I would never forget the anger on his face, a bitter anger—so bitter that I could almost taste it.

"Come with me," he said as he walked away. I followed and wondered again, *Where is he taking me?* I stepped into the boots at the top of the stairs, struggling to keep them on as I walked step-by-step down and out onto the yard. He stopped, turned to me, and asked where my soap and towel were.

"On me bed, sir," I replied, at which he withdrew the leather and beat me again across the shoulders, telling me to go back and get them. He was waiting as I returned shortly.

Glancing to my left, I saw a clock above a door, which I would later learn was the dining hall. The time was four-thirty, and I heard the clatter of boots and chatter of hushed voices. The classes were spilling out as boys hurried to their dormitories, came back out holding their towels, and lined up as I was led by Brother Cullen out onto the big, square, gravel yard. Some small buildings at one end were the shoemaker's shop, tailors' shop, and a shop where bed-springs were made. There were wooden benches lined along outside the last building. It was a cold February evening as I was told to put my clothes, towel, and soap on one of the benches. There were black shorts on the benches, and I was instructed to put on a pair and go into the showers. Sitting down, I started to take off my worn-out short pants, keeping an eye on the brother, who, in turn, was keeping focus on me as I slipped off my pants.

"Cover yourself!" he roared across at me.

I grabbed the little towel and attempted to cover my nakedness. It barely did. I saw him come closer with the leather in his hand, beating it against the side of his frock at every step, and then he stopped, looking down on me. As I pulled on the swimming shorts, he gave me a slap with the leather across my bare back.

"Come with me," he muttered, "and bring your soap."

I held my silence at the pain of the stinging, and I followed him to the building where the showers were.

"Go in there, turn on the tap, and use the soap to clean your dirty little body."

I turned on the tap, and the shock of the ice-cold shower, which was colder than the chilled February evening, took my breath away. *Colder than the River Shannon*, I thought, as it dulled the sting on my back. I rubbed the soap feverishly against my skin, trying to warm myself up, and saw the brother standing, watching me, but no matter how I rubbed, there was no sign of suds, and there was no hot water at all, just the ice-cold water to lather the piece of red carbolic soap. I thought, *This piece will last a while. Maybe that's why there is no hot water.* I came out of the shower shivering and walked out to the bench to my towel and clothes. My teeth were chattering by now. I dried myself with the piece of cloth that they called a towel. I had seen bigger hankies in Roache's stores on O'Connell Street. I put down the saturated towel and sat down on the bench to pull off the swimming trunks, making sure I put the wet towel across my still-wet lower body. Standing up, I put on the new short pants and quickly pulled the jumper on over my frozen hair. It was rough tweed to the touch. I pulled on the socks and stepped into the boots.

The lines of boys were coming up the yard, marching like soldiers with two Christian brothers walking behind. I was told to pick up my old clothes, my pants, and gansey, which was a soft sweater compared to the tweed. I took the wet towel and piece of soap and was told to go and stand by the wall, which I did, shivering from the cold wind blowing up off the river. The rest of the boys went through the same procedure, and I was told to get in line as they prepared to walk back to the dormitories. The crotch of the new pants rubbed roughly on my privates even though there was a piece of white, starched linen stitched over the fold in the middle, which afforded very little protection to my bare bottom. The following days would cause additional discomfort as the skin was rubbed almost raw.

Silence as we marched down the yard, and I was wary of even looking at the boy beside me for fear of further punishment when I heard him whisper, "Oh, sir, oh, sir, I am so sad," and then there was quietness again. I wondered what he was whispering about. I would ask him later when I got to know him. The walk was short. We stopped outside the dining hall in a drizzling rain and then we were allowed to go to our dormitories to put our towels on the rails of the beds to dry overnight and return to the yard to wait for supper.

We were walking around in circles and watched by a Christian brother, who was slapping his frock with his leather, just letting us know.

I spoke to the boy who had been whispering to me. "What were you saying to me coming from the showers?" I queried.

"You will know at supper later," he muttered, head down as we passed within hearing distance of the brother. "What's your name?" he wanted to know.

"Seanie. What's yours?"

"Jim. Why are you in here, Seanie?" he asked as we passed the tailor shop, continuing to circle with all the other boys.

"Mooching," I replied, "and I borrowed an old bike, but they said I stole it."

"Can you ride a bike?" he inquired.

"Yeah," I said proudly. "Why are you in here, Jim?"

He looked at me sadly and said his parents had died and he had been here for years. He said he couldn't remember how long. We fell silent again and glanced at the brother as he stepped closer to some of the boys in the front and whipped two of them across their backs for some unknown reason. But there was no sound out of them as they continued walking in circles. Every boy was underweight, I would later recall, including myself.

The following morning, having spent the night mostly awake and listening to the *clomp, clomp, clomp* every hour or so as the one-legged night watchman (Hoppy Dalton, his name was; I learned from Tim, another boy I got to know in Saint Columba's dormitory) and hearing the howl from a hunchbacked little man at dawn (Tom Toughy screaming, "I'll punch the devil out of you if you don't get up!") We washed our faces in the freezing-cold water in the wash-room. One small boy was crying profusely. As he did so, I asked him, "What's up with you?" He did not answer. The answer was later.

After we finished polishing the floors in the dormitory, we went to mass at six o'clock and ate the breakfast of porridge-gruel (no sugar), and a mug of milk in the dining hall at six-thirty, served by a boy (monitor) at each table as Brother Cullen turned on the big radio behind him at the top of the dining hall. We heard this was the BBC, a short bit of introduction music, and then the news. We spooned the thick, lumpy, undercooked gruel into our hungry mouths—no talking allowed until we were finished eating. Then we filed out into the still-early morning to walk in circles again in the exercise yard before classes. There he was, the little fellow. He must be about eight or nine, I thought, and I knew now why he was crying in the washroom. He was walking around with two other little boys, each with a mattress on their heads—they had wet their beds. It was very cold, and I wondered how their mattresses would dry. "They were denied breakfast," Jim reminded me while walking beside me as we circled the boys. "This is the way you are punished when you wet the bed," he continued, and we kept circling.

I asked about the "Oh, sir, oh, sir," thinking this was what he meant, but he said no.

"What did you think of your dinner?" he wanted to know.

"It was alright," I said. "I hadn't eaten for almost two days."

"Well," he said, "it will not fill you, and that's for sure." At which time Tim started to whisper with him, and a few other boys in front and behind joined in the hushed chant out of hearing of the brother,

"Oh, sir, oh, sir, I am so sad,
I got one spud, and that was bad,
I'm getting so skinny,
My shadow is gone,
And I'm nearly sure I won't live long.
Just one request before I go,
Who started this famine? I want to know.
May his ears turn green

And his nose turn blue
And the hairs on his head
His hat grow through,
And if there is any other disease he should chance,
May it be rheumatism and Saint Vitus dance."

At the mention of Saint Vitus dance, tears filled my eyes remembering my sister, Breeda, and at the same time, I avoided looking up from the graveled yard to not let them see a tear trickling down my face. I felt guilt at calling her names now that she and the others were taken away from me. I was lost in another world, it seemed.

I was thinking back to the dinner of minced meat and the potato and wondered if the food got worse. I had noticed that the minced meat smelled bad; rotten or something, and seen little white things in it. "Rice," I muttered.

"Those are maggots," one of the boys had proudly declared. But I and the others were hungry and ate them anyways as we would always do. Otherwise, you starved. We had to leave our plates clean, "Or else," we were told. Food could be stolen from the pigs that got the thrown-out food from the brothers' kitchen by Mary; boiled potatoes, cabbage, carrots, and stale bread—when they sent boys to the piggery to watch over them. When they had baby pigs, (we called them bonhams), they would send two trusted boys who they thought would not try to escape during the night—boys who had no parents or any family to go to. Jim and Tim would bring bits of pig's food back after a night there. Sometimes other boys were also given the job, mostly orphans though.

I was sent to a classroom that first morning and given papers with tests on them—math, writing, spelling, and what the brother called transcription and dictation. I must have looked a real fool sitting there wondering what he was talking about with dictation and transcription. I could read and write, but my math was not good. My spelling, however, was good. He assigned me to another classroom, which was about the same level I'd been at Creagh Lane in Limerick, and it was a level that I would stay in for the next few months until I reached the age of fourteen. Then I was selected to work in the cobbler's shop under the guidance of the shoemaker, who was tough but fair to us in the shop; fair if you kept your head down all day stitching leather uppers for the boots—tough if you did not.

Brother Cullen had written to my mother asking for my ration book and saying that she should send it to him. It was written on the back of a letter that I was supposed to have written to my mother; a letter that I would read at Aunt Nora's when I was released, and shake my head in disbelief.

It read,

> *St. Joseph's,*
> *Glin,*
> *Co. Limerick*
>
> *My dear Mother,*
>
> *Just a few lines hoping you are well. Mam I got your last letter and hope you got mine. Well Mam I am sorry I did not write sooner. I am writing now to ask you if you will send a storybook, two slabs of toffee and some biscuits, and hair oil. I also need a rack and a comb.*

I turned the page over, and on the back it said,

> *Please send John's ration book.*
>
> *Signed: JBC,*
>
> *Well Mam I have no more to say so good-bye.*
>
> *I remain your*
>
> *fond son.*
>
> *John.*

On the bottom of the page, it said,

Mrs. R. Morrison
No/ 10 Robert St.
Limerick.

My Mother Rose Plunkett, approximately age 18.

Of course, I had not written that letter as my letters from that time would not request anything from my poverty-stricken family. The letter was not in my handwriting either, so my mother would have seen that, and none of the requested items ever came, including the ration book, as far as I knew. I paid for that in the coming years working on the farm to supplement the lack of the ration book.

I was called from the cobbler's shop one day about June first or second, in 1949 and escorted by Brother Breen down to the chapel. As I stood before him there, he began to tell me of a sad occasion in my life. I stopped him talking by saying, "My sister is dead, isn't she?"

He looked at me in disbelief. "How did you know that?" he wanted to know.

"I dreamt of it last night," I told him.

I could see disbelief on his face.

I did not cry in front of him and reserved that for when I went to bed that night. Devastated at the news, I buried my head under the blanket and cried myself to sleep. I decided to write to my mother and let her know, but I had to be careful what I wrote as Brother Cullen read every letter before sending and you were allowed only one letter about every month. He went in the car to Limerick for whatever, for the brothers and other boys who had been committed. I was taken to Limerick for the funeral by Brother Cullen in the car, dropped off at our grandmother's house in Killeely, from where I would be taken to Saint Mary's Church to be asked if I wanted them to take the screws out of the coffin lid so I could view her. I refused to do that.

I was put in a horse-drawn carriage with my Aunt Maura and others of the family on my father's side. In a carriage behind came Rosaleen, Michael, and the baby. I was alone, it seemed, lost for words to my brothers and sisters, looking down as Breeda was laid to rest with her grandmother's aged sister, Molly Dear, in Saint Patrick's graveyard. My mother was either too sick or too upset.

I was taken back to Glin immediately after the funeral. My mother came to the institution to give me the little suitcase that she said was for me when I got out to join her in England. It was two weeks after Breeda's death and she said she was leaving for England. "She died of a broken heart," she said. "Don't worry, Seanie, I will send the fare for you to Nora's."

My sisters and brother were taken from our mother for neglect by the garda. They were led down William Street crying, and the baby was screaming for her mother, I learned. She was only six years old at the time as they were herded up to the police station to await the National Society for the Prevention of Cruelty to Children (NSPCC) to decide where they would be sent.

My cousins and sister Breeda with her head down. Myself, Mary Hourigan,
Rita Hourigan, Breeda Morrison, Peggy Hourigan, Noreen Hourigan.

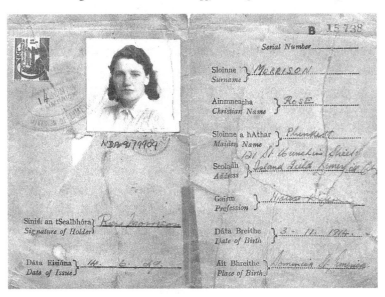

I did not see our mother again until I was nineteen years of age. She never came back to Ireland as far as I knew. Our mother's two sisters, Kitty and Nora, would ask for the children to be given to them, but the NSPCC said that our Aunt Nora was not well enough and Aunt Kitty worked and had no room for another five, which would be the case when I was released as well in the coming years. In any case, our Aunt Kitty worked all day up at the library in Pery Square, cleaning and stoking the boiler, sometimes helped by her daughters, Rita and Mary, the eldest two, who were a couple years older than me. The family lived out in Ballananty Beg over in Killeely, and the house had two bedrooms upstairs for the whole family, as we had in the Island Field. Uncle Paddy had the TB, and he and Kathleen, our aunt, had been living in a one-room flat with their three children above Marcella's fish-and-chip shop, next to the Thomond Cinema on Nicholas Street.

That left our grandmother, Bridget, who was called old Bridge by our mother. Mother said she called her that because we had to cross over the Thomond Bridge across the Shannon River from the island to get to her house, which she shared with our aunt Teresa and her husband, Francis. "Fra" would sit in front of the turf fire with his big boots on, and we would watch from the background in the cold kitchen as smoke rose from the burning soles of his boots, but whenever we visited, he would not move until our aunt Teresa put the food on the table.

I was already in Saint Joseph's Industrial school in Glin as my brother and sisters were taken in by our grandmother, and later in my life I would be horrified to hear of their account of life under the roof of that house. It was an account that they kept secret from me because of the shame; an account that our father would not hear of either, for what he might have done to avenge it, but that is a story that Rose, the baby, and Michael can only tell themselves.

The small black suitcase that my mother brought to Glin for me was taken by Brother Cullen and kept in the storage room to be given to me when I was to be released. When I took it on my way out, I would find some letters and notes inside the lid. I do not know why they were there. Maybe it was a place where my mother kept all her letters, I thought. One note was written on a piece of brown envelope. I could only assume it had been handed back to whoever handed it over or it had been placed there by Brother Cullen himself. It read,

Mrs. Morrisey, Munchin St. Limerick speaking.

Breeda Morrisey

Can Seanie Morrisey come home today as his sister is dead funeral 4 o'clock Guards will verify this. Will I go for him or will you send him by car.

Glin No. 7

(Glin Industrial School)

It looked as if it was written in pencil in good handwriting, with no signature or date, and if the brothers had only received it that day, then they would not have known that Breeda had died on the thirty-first of May, 1949, so I was wrong thinking that they had, for her funeral would be three days after she died. I was confused—my dream, the address on the piece of brown envelope (Munchin Street). Had I dreamed of her on the day she actually died, and was the name Morrisey, which I had learned from the Christian brothers, Morrison? We had always been called Morrisey on the island, but being called John was different, and I would get used to it.

I had written to my mother shortly before Breeda's death, recalling how Christy, Tiger, Dano Fitz, and Neddy Williams had attempted to see me but were refused. Christy's older brother was allowed and whispered to me when he came one Sunday to inform me and the brothers of the death of my Uncle Paddy, asking if I would be allowed to attend his funeral. Uncle Paddy had died of TB. I was refused permission.

Sitting in the classroom, I was allowed to write another letter to my mother, and this one was asking for money for the bus fare to Limerick Railway Station for a summer break, which we were encouraged to take in August as the brothers took their holidays in Kilkee, Jim had told me.

Saint Joseph's
Glin,
C/o Limerick.

Dear Mam,

Just a few lines hoping you are well. Well Mam I hope you know about the fare, it has gone up to a high price and it is in August we are going home. Well Mam Willy Drew came up on Sunday and told me about Paddy and I felt very sad so that is all I have to say for a while so good-bye hoping to hear from you soon. xxxxxxxx Best love for all the kids.

From your

Fond son

John. xxxxxx

I addressed the letter:

Mrs. Rose Morrison,
Saint Muinchin's St.
Island Field, Limerick.

Classroom at Glin Industrial School. Seanie in the centre third row from front.

I had misspelled Saint Munchin's St. Brother Cullen pointed out.

The superior had told us that the fare on the bus to Limerick and back to Glin was ten shillings, and I knew that was too much for our mother to send from wherever she was in England. I was resigned to catching spiders under the wall and eating their legs, which we believed would bring us good luck or maybe a miracle, I thought. We would stick out our tongues and the other boys would watch the legs wriggle before we swallowed them. I wondered if Aunt Nora would send my letter to my mother. Maybe she knew where she was in England.

I learned she had gone with Joe (her friend) two months after my sister Breeda died at our grandmother's house. I learned of her address from my Aunt Nora later, when she took me to have my passport (Travel Card) at that time and I kept in touch with her by letters.

Brother Murphy carried a tuning fork in the pocket of his black frock, and one day while we were required to sing in the classroom, he went from boy to boy asking that we go through the scale as he struck the fork against the desks, put it to his ear, and hummed the note. I was amused to learn that I had a voice at all, and he told me to stay behind one day after all the class left the yard. I went through the scale for an hour before he would let me go join them.

I was to sing in the choir from then on; sing for charity at halls around the countryside, Ballyhahill, etc.; sing solo at High Mass at Christmas (supported by two choirs); sing for everyone, it seemed, sing indeed. When I was eighteen years old and in England, Brother Murphy wrote to me after I'd written to him. In his response, he finished by saying, "You are still the thrush."

Brother Fitzmaurice taught catechism in the religious class and would beat it into you if you could not recite it at his commands. It took me quite some time to remember the whole book, but his torture was productive. I would grip the front of the desk and feel the terrible pain in my knuckles as the one-foot wooden ruler slashed down on them, almost severing them. I would watch his false teeth almost fall out with the force. For many of us it would take a long time to forget Brother Fitzmaurice and the religious teachings in Saint Joseph's Industrial School.

My education in the classroom came to an end that August 1949, and I thanked God for his pity as I was sent to the shoemaker's shop at age fourteen, to sit in silence all day long, stitching leather uppers for boot after boot, under the watchful eye of the shoemaker from the village, and spitting on the hemp and rolling it on the leg of my short pants. After two years they became very slick; polished with hemp and spittle.

I was told that a letter had been sent to my mother that previous month, July 1949, telling my mother of the pending summer vacation and all information pertaining to it.

Sgoil Seosaim Naomta
St Joseph's School
Gleann Corbraige,
Glin,
Co. Luimnige.

Co. Limerick.

July 1949

The summer Vacation will commence on Tuesday August 2nd

Kindly meet John at Limerick Railway Station on that date at 10:30am

The boys return on Thursday Sept. 1st by bus.

John is to be at Limerick Railway Station no later than 3:30 p.m. on that

date a brother will be there to meet him.

Fares :} Boys over 14 year's bus return Glin-Limerick 10/- shillings.

"Under" 14 years 5/- shillings

C.R Corcoran.

Superior.

All replies to be in before Saturday July 16th.

JBC.

I was under fourteen until the twenty-ninth but was told the fare was ten shillings. In any case, I was still resigned to eating spider legs, for even five shillings was insurmountable in my mind.

During this August month the dormitories were very cold and I cuddled under the blanket rolled up into a ball, rubbing my feet, trying to warm them. Most of the beds were empty, and I was terrified of being assaulted again during the night. I had woken one night and was startled to feel someone on top of me. I did not realize that it was one of the boys, who must have waited for Hoppy to do his rounds. I thought it was a brother as I had heard a couple of the boys whisper that they knew one of the brothers used to grope a few boys in the hen house after their beatings and also in the classroom sometimes. They would be sent to sit at the back of the class as you couldn't turn around in your desk during class. "Always face the blackboard," he would order.

I punched as hard as I could to dislodge the weight off me and was surprised to find it was the boy from the next bed on my side of the dormitory. He had an erection. I'd seen from the light from the bathroom that it was Tom, from the bed next to me. He was crying and said that he had been dreaming and "Please don't tell Hoppy, or he will kill me, and the brother will too." He didn't say which brother.

I just stared at him in disbelief as he climbed back into his bed, his head disappearing under the blanket. I heard him sobbing, and I would never mention that attack to anyone. I never spoke to Tom for the remainder of my time in Glin, but spent many nights lying awake, always aware of possible fondling until Tom was released and a new boy took his place.

I was unfortunate enough to be taken advantage of for the gratification of sexual desire by the brother who I suspected was molesting Tom. I was terrified to mention my concerns for fear of further beatings and prayed to the Virgin Mary like I had never prayed before in my life as I blamed myself for the attack. "Hail Mary, full of grace, the Lord is with thee. Blessed are thou amongst women, and blessed is the fruit of thy womb, Jesus. Holy Mary, mother of God, pray for us sinners now and at the hour of our death. Amen." It is a prayer that I've said every day of my life ever since.

The brother would sometimes come to my desk, and as he leaned down to look at my work, his hand would rub the inside of my bare leg as I kept my eyes closed and prayed until he moved back to the top of the class or left the room as we studied. Some boys glanced around, a sea of worried, sad eyes, day in and day out; some had been robbed of sleep as the dark circles showed and their gaunt expressions stared vacantly at one another.

One boy in particular sometimes muttered to himself. Sean wet the bed all the time. Stalky would beat him unmercifully every day after Tom Toughy inspected the beds before we went to Mass. Sean walked around the yard with his mattress on his head, ashamed, and he couldn't stop wetting the bed even though he was woken up every hour during the night by Hoppy.

Tommy had arrived at Glin and we talked as we met for the first time since I'd been sent in. He told me as we walked the yard that he'd stolen some oranges and that was why he was sent to Glin. Tommy's full name was Tommy DeLoughrey but we left out the De.

"Jasus, Tommy, we robbed every orchard, cleaned out more warehouses of oranges and tomatoes, and we never got caught. You missed me, didn't you?" I said, laughing for the first time in a very long time.

He just smiled back as we circled the yard. "Who is the lad with the mattress on his head, and why is he walking around with it?" he whispered.

"His name is Sean Lynch," I replied.

"Jasus, he looks awful."

"Quiet, Tommy, the brother might hear you. Tell me about the boys."

He told me that Tiger had taken a bike from outside the Craven "A" tobacco factory. There was Dano, Neddy, and Christy, and they had three bikes between the four of them. He said they were coming over the Sarsfield Bridge, and when they got back they told him all about it. "They were coming to see you," he said.

"Where were you?" I interrupted.

"I don't have a bike either, you know that, and I don't know how to ride one anyway."

"I forgot, Tommy. Go on. Now, what happened?"

"They said that as they cycled down towards Glin, they were stopped at Askeaton by the police. The police checked the numbers under the saddles. They wanted to know if the bikes were theirs, so they said they were, and the police let them go on their way. When they arrived at Glin, they'd seen some lads playing handball in the yard, and some of them had their heads shaved bald. They said they all were wearing boots, like what you are wearing, I suppose. Seanie, I've never seen you wearing boots before."

"I did have boots," I told him, "but they hurt my feet, and my mother pawned them at Pashy's. Do you remember the time we robbed the buns and hid in his doorway? Anyway, go on, what happened? Cause I never did see them here to visit me. Only Willie Drew came one Sunday about my Uncle Paddy's dying of TB."

"Well, let me finish, Seanie. They said that an old man asked them what they wanted," he continued, "and they all asked to see you. Christy said they were not allowed to speak to any of you. They were led away to a sort of kitchen with a long wooden table and seat. They were given a mug of milk and a slice of bread and then told to be on their way. That's why you've never seen them, Seanie Morrisey, and I found out Sean Bourke was sent to Daigenen in Dublin for robbing the bananas out of the car and not sent here at all like we were told."

"I know, Tommy, I looked for him here meself and I haven't seen him. There's only you and me, Tommy, and two brothers; the Sheehan boys, Tom and Pat. They said they have well-off American cousins living in Limerick. They came all the way over from America a while ago. I know I would love to be in America. Joe Louis lives over there, and I have uncles and aunts over there too."

It was Sunday morning, and Mass was over. We had our porridge and milk and said grace after the meal as we had said grace before the meal, as usual. We filed out into the damp, cold morning air, realizing that we would go for our walk through the countryside, which we all looked forward to each weekend. We walked in silence down the steep hill that was Glin, which was lined with little shops and smaller houses, as the townsfolk were coming and going from Mass in the village church. They watched us with sympathetic looks on their faces as our group of about twenty in pairs followed the brother, who kept a cautious look back every now and then, making sure we stayed close together. It would be foolish to try and run, I thought, you would not get far, especially in the daytime. You would have to take the road to Limerick one way or the road to Kerry the other way, along the River Shannon, the County Clare on the opposite side of the river at this wide juncture in the fast and cold water as it entered the Atlantic Ocean a short distance further on.

There would be a time and different circumstance to let thoughts of escape from this awful institution fester in my tormented mind, and I was sure that others were thinking similar thoughts as we wheeled right at the bottom of the hill this Sunday; one of two routes that were available to us. The berries and leaves on the bushes during this time of year were a joy to those with fast hands, making sure that the brother did not see you. We called the edible berries and leaves "bread and cheese." The berries were ripe, red, and soft with a tiny stone in the center, and the tender, serrated leaves were filling to a stomach, which would be the size of my fist, I suppose. Easy to please, I recall. We were not chastised as we walked and talked away out of the village,

and the brother would sometimes point out when he wanted silence, sometimes coming back behind the group and again moving forward. We kept a steady pace as we covered about six miles, rain or shine, away from the confines of the place of suffering for so many. Yet it was the only home for quite a lot of the unfortunate orphans sentenced to suffer with criminals such as myself, and I wondered why. The walk back was always at a slower pace as we tried to prolong the stay in what was freedom outside the walls, our bellies full of berries and leaves and even some smiles on rose-coloured faces, but smiles that would disappear as we entered the stone-grey confines again.

"Who are all these people?" a few of the newer inmates would inquire as we stared at a procession of older people walking around the school grounds, guided by white-cloaked orderlies. Some of these people were pulling faces, others crying while looking at them, and yet others were laughing for no apparent reason.

"They're from the madhouse in Limerick, and they are the sane ones," Jim told me. "They come here often for their walks away from the lunatic asylum, I was told, but they don't bother us. They just look. Maybe they think we are mad too. Maybe we are." He laughed and then walked away toward the lavatories in the yard.

"Where are you going?" I asked.

"To the lav," he said.

"Watch that the brother doesn't catch you. No smoking butts in the lav," I reminded him. He smiled.

The surprise inspections came often, with everyone ordered to stand in the center of the yard. You were required to stand still with your hands out in front of you. A brother would start walking the lines of boys, stopping in front of each one, ordering that you pull out your pants pockets. God help you if a cigarette butt fell out on the ground. You could feel the tension in the air as you hoped no one was caught. The cigarette butts used to be picked up on our walks on the Sundays, whether they were wet or dry, and they were mostly wet, soggy, well-smoked fags that the smoker dropped after his fingers started to burn. Sometimes a few butts would be found in the discarded slops Mary sent from the brothers' kitchen for the pigs, so those who smoked not only had the best picking from the slops but a few butts as well.

Blacky was a big boy and was nearing being released as he pulled out his pockets for the brother; a new young brother, who must have been about eighteen years old or older, I thought. A look of surprise came across the brother's face as he looked down at a cigarette stump at his feet. He asked Blacky for an explanation. Blacky answered that he did not smoke and did not know how the stump got there, as the brother was removing the white collar from his neck. This was a sign that he was acting outside his calling as a Christian brother. He put his collar in the pocket of his habit, told Blacky to follow him into the exercise hall, and ordered us to stay in line until he came out. Some minutes passed as we heard scuffling and panting. Eventually, after about ten minutes or more, the young brother came out reattaching his collar and followed by an unscathed Blacky. The brother's right eye was red and puffed a little. Blacky walked back to our line and had a smile on his face. The brother dismissed us and left the yard, walking back toward the brothers' quarters and the kitchen.

I did not see Blacky around after that. He was gone—gone from the school, we were told, to work for a farmer somewhere in Kerry. The brother who had fought him in the exercise hall, his right eye now black, was soon to leave also, but we did not miss him. Another would take his place to follow in his footsteps, watching us all the time as we played murder ball on the concrete floor in the hall, an exercise reserved for the rainiest of days, as we played Gaelic football on finer days.

Soon it was apparent to the brothers that Tommy and I were acting like close friends as we spent a lot of time talking in the yard, circling around during our after-school and workshop or farm duties. We were called aside individually and questioned as to our relationship before arriving at Glin. I told the brother that Tommy and I were living on the same street in the Island Field and had grown up together. I do not know what Tommy said, but we were ordered to not be seen together from then on. We dared not, even in the same classroom. It would be almost sixty years before I would get to talk to him again on the phone, an instrument that was not known to me in those days. He died shortly after.

Time was the essence to me. I was lying awake in my bed, a distraction from the cries, moans, and coughing heard from other parts of the dormitories—cold, damp dormitories. And I put myself back mentally to my earlier days in the city, thirty-two miles away. I imagined walking all the way back, kicking off the Glin boots with the nails sticking up through the soles, and feeling the soft, wet grass on the side of the road, caressing my bare feet again. I thought of being able to wipe my nose on the sleeve of my gansey, walking free, away from this sadistic hellhole. I would arrive on the dock road, and there, lying all over, would be big pieces of coal; coal that I would put in the old pram that I found at the Corkenree dump. Mind you, one or two of the wheels would be wobbly, but that was all right. It wasn't far now to Robert Street, I thought. I would love to go to Sparling's little shop on Nicolas Street first and buy a bag of dilix, my favorite seaweed, for a halfpenny and, with the other halfpenny in the one good pocket of my pants, ask her for a pint of winkles. *Wouldn't that be grand now?* I thought. A big roaring coal fire and our bellies full, and the rats would choke on the smoke, I would laugh to myself. We only had one pin between all of us for the winkles, but I pulled the snail out slowly, ever so slowly, as he wound his way out of his little shell impaled on the pin, a soft, salty taste of the cold Atlantic Ocean caressing our pallets as we sat on the bed mesmerized by the dancing flames. Our mother would be singing softly as the kettle boiled over the fire, and Breeda, Rosaleen, Michael, and the baby all waiting for the pin. "You are only supposed to eat one and give us the pin, Seanie Morrisey," they would call out, and I would say sorry as I handed over the pin. I opened the newspaper page filled with fresh dilix. Some said that the seaweed had every known vitamin known to man. I wondered what *vitamins* meant, but it tasted better than the seaweed off the rocks at Glin,

I would muse—seaweed that the brothers didn't know we stole off the Shannon slippery rocks on our swims—green seaweed, not like Sparling's, beautiful brown, salty, and crispy.

I awoke to, "The devil out of you," as the hunchback slapped on the iron bed frames on his way through the dormitory, and I could see his breath in the dim light as I put my feet on the ice-cold polished floor, keeping the one thin blanket covering myself as I reached for my pants on the foot of the bed. *Jesus, Mary, and Holy Saint Joseph, I'm famished,* I thought and remembered my thoughts the previous evening—no coal fires here and no dilix or periwinkles either, and my stomach ached at the very thought of food. I washed my face in the freezing water in the washroom. There was some toilet cleaning powder on the shelf above the basin. I put some on my finger and rubbed my teeth. It tasted awful, but I knew I had to look after my teeth. I didn't want the man they called the dentist yanking out my teeth with the pliers in the dispensary and the thought of the deformed hands of the big nurse holding me down as she kept saying, "Will ye hush now," to the boys in the chair as they kicked and yelled over the bucket of blood at their feet. Jim told me that he had struggled to get out of the clutches of the nurse and, in doing so, kicked the bucket up in the air, spilling blood all over the walls and getting an unmerciful beating for doing so.

It was summer now, and the potatoes were ready for picking out of the fields. I was taken out of the shoemaker's shop and joined the other boys. The two horses were harnessed to the plow, and Bob, the farmhand, had hold of the reins as we lined up at the field, all the time watching the brother leaning on his blackthorn walking stick, an evil look in his dark eyes. I had the feeling he was watching me farther down the line of boys. There was an order from Bob for the horses to "Go, boys" as they strained on the harness. No whip needed with them either. They were better treated than us, I thought, thinking how Brother K seemed to enjoy beating me with the walking stick at any chance he thought fit, like when he had me alone in the onion field and caught me nibble on one of the green onions that I was weeding. The shock of the heavy blackthorn across my back as I knelt in the rows brought tears to my eyes, and it wasn't from the onions, I was telling a couple of the boys.

They knew very well what Brother K could and would do and smiled at the onion crack. "I just hope he never calls me on my own to do jobs for him," one of them said.

"For some reason, he does not like me," I whispered, seeing him looking my way again.

"Just cry when he beats you. He won't stop if you don't cry."

"I won't give him the pleasure," I muttered.

"Well, look out then," the boy nearest me continued. "He is a bad brother. He loves that stick."

On one occasion, Brother K had me come up to feed the calves. I followed him from the shop to the stables where one of the boys who worked on the farm had just milked some cows. "Pick up those two buckets of milk, and follow me," he instructed as he walked ahead. I was careful not to spill any of the milk, and I fell behind a little as I walked over the rough ground up the field. I was surprised he did not come back and beat me for being so slow. *Maybe he is easing up,* I thought and hoped as I reached the gate where he stood looking at the five calves in the distant field standing and looking our way.

He opened the gate and told me to go in the field with the buckets. "And don't spill a drop! Or God in Heaven help you," he yelled as he held the stick high over his head.

So much for easing up, I thought. He had a sadistic look as I walked past him carrying the milk buckets. He closed the gate behind me and put his foot on the bottom board of the gate as I saw the calves come racing toward me. They were hungry for their milk, and I was like a magnet holding the two buckets. "Stand still!" was all I heard as the stampede hit me, knocking me back against the gate. I looked up and saw the brother's grinning face. For some unknown reason, the buckets had not tipped over as the calves stuck their heads around me, sucking out of them. He seemed to enjoy the scene, and I was hurting from the surprise of it all, still holding on to the buckets.

There were other little chores on the farm. Backs bent, we began to follow the horse-drawn plow as it turned the soil over, exposing the potatoes. We picked them feverishly, putting them in the sacks. To our amusement, little field mice were scurrying all around us, running in all directions, also in the hay gathering.

We went back to our workshops, shoemaking, tailoring, and making bedsprings as summer turned toward winter. Those under fourteen were back to their classes of Gaelic and religion, again waiting for the opportunity to return to the fields and a little freedom from the classrooms and shops of silence. I liked the hay gathering as we stooped in a long line and could chat freely as the noise of the machine moved ahead cutting the hay, with corncrakes and field mice scattering in every direction. We kept both our hands open in a sweeping motion like rakes, making little haystacks on our way through the field. The only bad thing about it was the stings from the thorns of the thistles in our hands, but everyone seemed happier anyway. We could chat and laugh at the antics of the corncrakes in their panic to escape the blades of the machine, and we could forget for a while.

I was walking in the yard; it was a Saturday evening, I recall. The brother noticed me talking to one of the boys as the chapel bell rang the Angelus. I did not see him approach, and the crack of the leather across my legs caused me to fall to the ground. I saw his soft-leather black shoe coming at my head, but it struck the gravel stones first, sending a hail of small stones into my face. The pain in my right eye was excruciating, as if a sharp, hot knife had been plunged into it. I was blinded, both eyes shut as I scrambled to my feet, not hearing a sound except for the bell. I stood still wondering what was next, and then I felt a rough hand grabbing my shoulders and heard the brother telling me, "Open your eyes and look at me."

"I can't, sir," I cried.

He must have seen the trickle of blood coming from the corner of my right eye. He led me to the recreation hall, guided me to one of the wooden benches, and had me sit down. I could feel his hands shaking as he tried to open my eye. He then led me to the infirmary, where the nurse forced open my eye to look at it. I heard her say that I would have to go to a doctor as she did not have the proper equipment in the infirmary and she asked the brother to go and get Brother Cullen as he could drive the car. I was taken a short distance in the car, to where I learned was the little town of Tarbert, and led into a house where a doctor lived.

The doctor asked what happened, and I heard Brother Cullen in the next room telling him that the yard was covered in gravel and the boys played rough sometimes and this was what had happened. The doctor looked through a glass into my eye and said a little stone was stuck in the pupil and laughed, saying to Brother Cullen, "Isn't that the truth? A stone stuck in a pupil." They both laughed at that. After some painful poking around in my eye, he said he got it out and told me to put a patch over my eye and to be more careful playing on the gravel. I looked at him through blurred eyes and then looked at Brother Cullen, who thanked the doctor and led me back to the car, driving back the three miles to Glin.

I decided that I must escape no matter to where. I had slept under bushes before, and I was a good beggar. I had lots of experience at that. *Anywhere would be better than here*, I thought. When my eye had gotten better, I would go. I would lie awake at night and go through how I would get away and only having regrets of leaving the other boys and, especially, the choir and the protection of Brother Murphy, who called me "the thrush." I was his little tenor, he would say.

The night watchmen had left the dormitory for the third time that night as I lay in bed. I was already dressed under the blanket, and I slid out of the bed and crawled on hands and knees past the sleeping boys, making my way down the stairs and out into the yard, not bothering to get my boots and socks, making my way slowly down the long driveway and into the field away from the gate, climbing over the wall onto the country road. I started to run, feeling the thrill of freedom as I distanced myself from the school in the pitch-black night. I eventually saw a barn and wandered in, hearing the barking of a dog in the distance, and I hoped that he would not wake the farmer. I was wet and tired and fell asleep on the pile of hay in the barn, which I shared with a donkey nearby. The sound of a cock crowing woke me, and I wondered if there were hens as well. I would love to taste a real egg. I had forgotten what they tasted like as we only got one egg a year at Easter.

My luck was in as I found a fresh egg in the corner of the barn, and it was still warm to the touch. I held it in my trembling hands and wondered how to open it, tapping it against the side of the wood and spilling half of it as it cracked open, but I sucked the remainder into my mouth as the donkey stood watching me. "You can have the other half," I said to him. I made my way out of the barn, glancing around to make sure I was not spotted, only to encounter the big old, friendly farm dog blocking my way. I spoke softly to him and showed him my open palm, just to make sure he'd seen I was friendly too. His head went down, and his big bushy tail waved from side to side. "Good boy." I called him "Tuppence," not knowing his name. He did not seem to mind as I walked past him, and he started to follow me to the road in the cool dawn, stopping at the entrance to the little farm gate as I continued past and on my way to my freedom, or so I thought at that time.

It would have been known by now that I was missing, and I was sure that they would have told the garda, so I kept off the road, and that slowed me down as I had to climb over stone walls and through bushes in every field, sometimes cutting my knees on the sharp stones. I wondered, *How far to Limerick now? Will I ever get there? Where will I go to when I get there?* No one had come to see me since I was sent, except for Willy Drew and my mother on her way to England. I thought that maybe I could go and knock at a farmer's door and ask if he needed someone to help on the farm. Then I smiled to myself and thought about the song, "The Farmers Boy" and began to sing to myself as I scurried from hedgerow to hedgerow, field by field. "The sun went down beyond the hill across the dreary moor when tired and lame boy there came up to a farmer's door. Could you tell me if one there be, that here you would employ, to plough and sow and reap and mow to be a farmer's boy, to be a farmer's boy. My father's dead, my mother's left with five poor children, small, and what is worse for Mother is, I'm the eldest of them all."

I stopped singing. *This is too real,* I thought. *It must have been composed for me, but I'm not knocking on any farmer's door.*

Then I heard talking on the road just ahead. I stood stock-still, not even wanting to breathe, hearing, "There he is, over by the bushes."

I knew that it was useless to run back. The road to Limerick was not on my mind anymore. I knew what to expect back in Glin and resigned myself to the punishment, walking over to the garda on the road. He asked me my name.

"Seanie Morrisey, sir."

"Would that be John Morrison now, boyo?"

Begrudgingly I said, "'Tis sir."

"Well, Seanie or John, the brothers are very worried about you and asked me to find you and bring you back to Saint Joseph's. You must be starving, and you look like a drowned dog. Why in the name of heavens did you run away from Saint Joseph's? Surely it is not that bad a place. All the other boys don't run away. Do you have parents? Is that why you ran?"

I just hung my head down, and he led me to the car.

I had not got very far as it took very little time to reach Glin and Saint Joseph's.

"This is the second time that you have been escorted into Saint Joseph's, and it will, hopefully, be your last," the superior brother remarked as the garda walked away, getting into the car. The superior thanked him for "returning this troubled boy to the school. Some boys do not appreciate what we do for them."

"God bless you, brother, for all the good work you do," the garda said as he drove away out of the school gate.

The hair was falling all around me as the brother hacked away with the scissors, sometimes cutting my scalp until I was almost bald, except for the little tufts that I felt later as I lay in bed. There were no mirrors, so I could only feel with my hands, and I wondered what I looked like. I waited the next morning to be taken to the superior and to receive the instructions that I expected. "You will go to the shoemaker's shop and continue your duties. You will not look at anyone there, and when you leave the shop, you will keep your head down in shame. You will not look at anyone, and if you do, you will be severely punished. Now get out of my sight. You have brought shame on everyone here."

I was called from the shop that same day by Brother Murphy. He was devastated, he said, that I would do such a thing, and he asked that I promise never to run away again. I promised. As I looked at the ground, he gave me a paper with a hymn written on it and told me that I was to study it while doing my penance for my running away. "It will be a Gregorian Christmas this year," he continues, "and this hymn was written around 1274 by Saint Thomas Aquinas, 'Bread of Angels' or 'Panis Angelicus.' Read it, and I will listen to you sing it when you are ready." He led me back to the shoemaker's shop. "Fecking bread of angels, is it? What about bread of fecking Glin?" I blurted out in the corner of the shop as I stitched an upper, getting a sideway glance from the boy sitting next to me.

"Shush," he whispered. "They will kill you. You are not supposed to talk."

The shoemaker had not heard me. I assumed he was using the machine finishing a boot. I nodded and continued stitching.

"How far did you get?" he whispered.

I looked toward the shoemaker and, seeing him busy, said, "About ten miles, I think, not far enough."

I sat in the exercise hall before our meal reading the hymn, sitting by two other boys, who were also bald and with their heads bowed. They had run away a week before on horseback and were caught also. One of them raised his head to look at what I was reading and was spotted by the brother. The brother gave him a terrible beating about the head as I crumpled the hymn in anger. I was as helpless as they were, and all the other boys playing murder ball stopped and stared in our direction before being told to "Get back to your game, or you will sit with these shameless articles."

I read the hymn a hundred times as I finished my penance and Brother Murphy said that it was time to practice singing it. I listened to Brother Cullen playing the piano as I stood by and sang until I got it right after what seemed an eternity.

Panis Angelicus, fit panis hominum,
Dat panis caelicus, figuris terminum,
O res mirabilis, manducat Dominum
Pauper, Pauper, servus, et humilis.
Pauper, Pauper, servus, et humilis.

At High Mass in the village of Glin that Christmas, accompanied by our choir and the men's and ladies' choir from the village, I sang that part of "Bread of Angels" solo, and the choirs continued the rest of the Gregorian chant or hymn following.

Te Trina Deitas, unaque poscimus,
Sic nos tu visita, sicut te colimus,
Per tuas semitas, duc nos quo tendimus,
Ad lucem quam inhabitas,
Amen.

I was to sing almost every day now under the guidance and tute-lage of Brother Murphy, and I was avoiding the usual beatings most of the other boys were dealt. The choir was off bounds, it seemed now, and we performed in many of the little villages around the county. We were sometimes treated with a biscuit or two at the back of the stages.

One day, as I reached the age of about fifteen and a half, there was a large gathering in the brothers' quarters. We played Gaelic-league football in the field in front. I was called over to the dance by Brother Murphy in the middle of the game, and the rest played on. He struck the tuning fork on the post, held it to his ear, and hummed the note to me, and I knew what was required, so I started to sing the usual practice song, which was the "Bells of Shandon," which I never figured, as Brother Murphy was from Dublin. In fact, he'd once kissed the film star Maureen O'Hara on the stage in a play in Dublin, he bragged. He would always tell us who wrote the songs and when. This one was Francis Mahoney's, 1805-1866, he had told us. I think that Francis Mahoney took a long time to write that one, I had said earlier to one of the choir.

"But surely, it must be his lifespan," he replied, puzzled.

We all laughed when we later were on our own. That crossed my mind as I began to sing.

> With deep affection, and recollection,
> I oft times think of those Shandon bells,
> Whose sounds so wild would,
> In the days of childhood,
> Fling round my cradle
> Their magic spell.
> On this I ponder
> Where'er I wander,
> And thus grow fonder,
> Sweet Cork, of thee,

With thy bells of Shandon,
That sounds so grand on,
The pleasant waters,
Of the River Lee.

"That's grand, Sean. No need to sing the rest. Your voice is in fine form. There are people here from Dublin who want you to sing for them shortly."

I got a little nervous at that and was led into the brothers' lounge, where there was some recording equipment set up and a microphone nearby. I was given a glass of water and asked to step up to the microphone and to take a deep breath before singing to silence. There was just the rustle of a brother's frock as I repeated singing the "Bells of Shandon." To my horror, my voice started to break on the high note—a quiver, it seemed, had pierced the air. I was becoming a man—first the voice breaking, and I knew that soon I would be released into a new world, and the choir, boy by boy would follow me. It would be like coming out of a tainted cocoon, spreading our wings, and flying away from this hellhole. Brother Murphy consoled me over losing my voice, saying that it would soon become stronger, as if I cared one way or another. I would never sing another note, I thought. They were voice robbers, however, I respected Brother Murphy for his kindness. I was kept in the choir until my release but kept from singing solo anymore.

The time was fast approaching to my sixteenth birthday. I was just sewing leather in the shoemaker's shop and was allowed to talk, being prepared for the outside, but the damage had already been done, and no amount of kindness would blot out the memories already implanted in my soul.

I was expecting to go to England to my mother when I got out, but there was a twist to that. One day, out of the blue, my long-gone father arrived at the school and was given permission to take me out into the countryside for a walk and talk. He cut a branch off a tree as we strolled through the fields and placed it on his shoulder. As we talked, I continually called him sir. He said not to call him sir as he was my father. I kept replying "sir," and said, "I am sorry, Dad." That was the hardest word I had to say, I recalled later.

Suddenly, he brought the stick down with such force close to my shoulder that I waited for impact. My heart almost stopped. There at my feet, a rabbit, its back broken, kicked out in its final moments.

"You can have him for your dinner," he informed me.

I looked at him in disbelief, but I would not tell him what we were fed. It certainly was not rabbit for dinner. He picked up the dead rabbit, and we continued walking. I felt uneasy in his company as I had not seen him in such a long time and was grateful for his taking me back to the school, showing the rabbit to the brother, and asking him to have it cooked for me and my friends after he skinned it and cleaned it out. He left shortly after, and the rabbit was boiled by one of the boys who worked in the kitchen. I went to dinner that day, and the rabbit was brought out by the same boy to our table, which was next to the kitchen. We tried to chew the meat and gave up; it was rock hard, and as I was the monitor of the table, I went and got the usual mincemeat and potato for each boy. "You boiled it too long," I told the kitchen boy and smiled. "But never mind," I assured him. "It was too rich for us anyway."

A big grin spread across his face. "I know how to boil mincemeat," he said.

"You certainly do, and the rice in it too," I said, smiling as I left the kitchen.

It would be many years later that I learned what had transpired in July 1951, a month before I was set free from Glin. The letter, written by Brother Cullen read,

Sgoil Seraim Naomta,	*St. Joseph's School*
Gleann Corbraige	*Glin*
Co. Luimnige.	*Co. Limerick*
	11.7.51

Dear Mrs. Morrison,

Your letter received and noted. John will finish here on the 28th August next, and the superior would like to know what you intend doing with him. John is doing very well, and he himself is anxious to know if you intend taking him to England or not.

Yours sincerely,

J.B Cullen

(For Supr.)

August 28, 1951, came. It was late morning. I said good-bye to the shoemaker, noticing tears in his eyes as I walked from the shop. I looked back at the other two boys sitting on the bench, and it troubled my heart, but at the same time, I was excited to be on my way out at last. I was taken by Brother Cullen to the store, and he had me put on a new jacket and short pants. I was given new boots and socks, no identity tags on the socks now, and he said that he would take my picture, which he did. I had already filled my pockets with my little possessions, which I had saved over the duration, mostly religious items—rosary beads, little prayer book, etc., from my discarded old jacket. I was holding the little suitcase my mother had brought me tightly in my hands.

I was taken to the brother superior's quarters, where he informed me that I was being taken to the house of my father's mother— my grandmother's, he corrected. He had not heard back from my mother, he told me, and my father had set up a good job for me in Limerick City, where I would be working for a Mrs. Ryan, and it was close to the house over in Kileely. I wondered why my mother had not come for me, and I was disappointed. She had promised to take me to England. It was only then that I remembered my brother and sisters and wondered about them. I had forgotten their faces since February 1949. I was looking forward to seeing them again and resigned myself to being with them again. Would they remember me, I wondered. What with my new boots and new clothes, they would wonder who I was.

Being released age 16, 1951.

I was leaving in Brother Cullen's car, without seeing any of my friends or Brother Murphy. I was driving away from one life and into another and was amazed that I was upset as I watched the gate close behind us. It should have been the happiest moment of my life, but it was not—I was confused.

The journey took about an hour before we entered the city limits, and already I was eager to get out of the car and walk through the streets that I had forgotten.

We pulled up outside the house on Cregan Avenue, Kileely, and I immediately was surrounded by children all looking in at me, excited. The news had gone around that I was on my way there. Brother Cullen came around the car and opened the door. My grandmother stood at the door of the house, her shawl drawn around her as she came down the steps toward me and the brother, a big grin on her face, showing me the one tooth. "Come here, Seanie, and give poor Nana a big hug. We missed you all this time."

"Look after him, Mrs. Morrison. He is a fine boy."

I was almost wrapped up in the black shawl as I gave the brother a look of disbelief as he got back into the car and drove away. The family were all excited. Rosaleen was the eldest sister now; she was going on twelve years of age, and like a mother to Michael and Frances. They kept looking at me as I sat by the fireplace with a mug of steaming tea in my hands. I had not tasted tea in almost three years.

"Seanie, will you take me for a ride on the bike?" Michael blurted out.

I looked at him. "I will, indeed. I'll have to pump up the tires though," I said laughing.

"The deaf and dumb man next door, Abba, has a bike, Seanie. If you get cigarette butts for him, he will lend it to you."

"And where would I be getting butts from now, Michael?"

"He has a cart with pram wheels on it, and we could pick up butts from all over town for him."

"And what does he do with the butts?" I asked.

"He rolls cigarettes out of them and sells them," Michael replied.

"What's the cart for? Are there that many butts lying around the streets now?"

"That's not what it's just used for, it's also for bundles of sticks that he sells too. I lie on my stomach in the cart while you push it, and I pick up the butts as we go around the town. Pa Byrnes doesn't come with me very much now, so you can. Will you, Seanie?"

I agreed to give it a try. I soon learned the sign language, and Abba was pleased with our help. Michael and Frances had rides on the bike, on the crossbar, to their delight. Rosaleen wasn't too keen though.

Our father was in England, as well as our mother, and we were sharing flea-ridden beds at our grandmother's. I realized then that they were like the fleas in our beds at Glin. I wondered when I was getting the job I was supposed to have that my father had said to the brothers. I was getting restless just pushing a cart around Limerick looking for cigarette ends. Michael was always at our Aunt Kitty's. She fed him, he told me. I spent most of the time at my Aunt Nora's in the Island Field. That was where I could write to my mother in England without being questioned by our grandmother and Aunt Teresa, about my mother. They had a dim view of her for leaving Ireland with Joe. "Sonny Morrison, your father, treated your good-for-nothing mother very well, and will you have a look what she's done to him behind his back, and your sister Breeda not yet cold in her grave. God have mercy on her."

I exploded on my grandmother. "Don't call my mother names!" I screamed at her. She was shocked at my reaction, pulled her shawl on, and walked out the door. I think I frightened her. I had been subdued in Saint Joseph's for too long, and the temper flared that day. I regretted that and apologized to her when she came back.

Our father came home for a week and took me to Mrs. Ryan's yard about a mile from our grandmother's and I could smell the pigs from a distance. He introduced me to Mrs. Ryan. "Seanie has great experience with pigs," he told her. I gave him a sideways glance, expecting him to tell her I just got out of Glin. I was ashamed to have been in Glin and did not want to have everyone know I had been sent there. He never mentioned it to her, and I was relieved.

She offered me the job. She said, "We have thirty pigs and a few geese. You know they have to be fed and the sties kept clean. You know how to ride a horse, your father tells me. Well, the horse is kept up in the field just up the road, and you will have to harness him up to the cart and go into town to a couple of hotels for the slops, cooked and uncooked, in the two forty-five-gallon barrels.

"There's a big kettle where the raw slops will have to be cooked. There is plenty of wood to burn, and you will have to make sure that there is no broken glass or broken bottles in the cooked food. It would not be good, now, if the pigs ate the glass, would it?"

"How will I know that, Mrs. Ryan?"

"Just feel with your hands," she replied.

I said nothing, thinking *What about my hands?* "All right, Mrs. Ryan," I assured her.

"Now will ten shillings a week be too much?" She winked at my father.

"Oh no, Mrs. Ryan, that will be fine." I was glad to have a job at last, and I had never had ten shillings before.

I started enjoying the work and soon was picking up children on the horse and cart on their way to school in the mornings. The horse was very cranky and let me know he did not approve of the extra load of kids sitting on the cart. He would kick and snort but settled down when I dropped the children at the school ground as I carried on to the hotels.

One morning, to my great surprise and joy, Jim came out to the back of the Glenworth Hotel with a bucket of slops to drop in the drums. We looked at each other in disbelief. "Jim!" I shouted in my excitement. "What in the name of heaven are you doing here?"

"Hello, Seanie," he said as his eyes lit up. "What are you doing here yourself? I thought you were gone to England with your mother months ago."

"I don't know what happened at all, Jim, but they gave me to my father as he told them he had this job for me."

"When did you get out? It's lovely seeing you again. I was wondering how you and the boys were. John McGragh is here too," he went on.

"Well that's great news, Jim. Where's John? I'd love to see him again. I missed you both after you got out. They let me out this August, and I stay at my grandmother's house. How do you and John like this hotel job?"

"A little better than school, for sure, Seanie. But you would not believe the way they treat us here. We are still slaves."

Just then a man came out and ordered Jim back into the hotel. "I would be obliged if you did not gab to the boys," he rasped at me. "Get the slops and be on your way."

It played on my mind as I drove back to Mrs. Ryan's laden with the two big drums of slops, looking at them, and thinking what a treasure trove this would have been in Glin.

Weeks went by, and I was not seeing Jim or John at the hotel. I was afraid to get them into trouble in case they were sent back to Saint Joseph's. Jim had been in Glin a lot longer than me. I could not get Glin out of my mind—starving boys freezing through the coming winter for the lack of warm bedding and clothing. At least I had an overcoat now, a bit too big, but it was like a blanket to cover myself and my brother as well. Sadly, I would be warmer than the boys. We boiled the kettle on the fire at our grandmother's house to wash our faces; not so in Glin. I remembered putting all the little bits of soap into an urn and melting them into a solid bar and cutting it into small bars, bars that barely made a bubble. This going through my mind as I felt through the uncooked slops for glass before putting it in the big urn to cook; potatoes, dead cabbage, parsnips, and carrots all rotting as

I stirred the slops with the wooden paddle, throwing firewood under and feeling the heat as I stood on the platform by the open window of the shed, seeing the four pigs snorting around where I dumped the water out of the urn into the little farm field next door. Several times, I had watched the pigs rooting for pieces of food that were in the water bucket as I emptied the urn, and I began to dislike the big saddleback boar. He pushed the smaller sows away and was very greedy. I thought, *I would kick him if I could get near him.* Having fed the pigs with great difficulty, coming to the door of the sties with the buckets of slops to be greeted by some of them with their hooves on top of the half doors, I had to put the buckets down and start punching them on the snouts in order to get the door open. Mrs. Ryan saw me one day and told me not to punch the pigs as it would leave blue marks on them when slaughtered. One huge sow had bonhams, which are baby pigs, and was in a corner sty. I used to have a pitchfork in one hand and a bucket in the other. She was glaring at me when I went to feed them, but I felt safe holding the fork like a spear.

The day would wind down around six o'clock as I cleaned the sties and put fresh straw down, emptying the wheelbarrow full of pig shite in the pit up the yard through the big gates several times. The big geese would always want to come out as I opened the gates. I had a struggle chasing them back and closing the doors behind me. One day as I got through, one of the ganders stood straight up; he was as big as me, hissing and spitting at me. I picked up a stone at my feet and let fly, hitting him square on the head. He wobbled, blood visible through the feathers, and staggered back up the yard. The next day, Mrs. Ryan wanted to know what happened to the gander as he was dead, blood on his head.

"I will tell you, Mrs. Ryan, there was an awful fight between the two of them, and I'm sure that that one over there," I was pointing to the poor innocent goose, "did it." *I have to tell the priest at confession on Saturday,* I thought. *It's a venial sin to lie about that, but Mrs.*

Ryan would *let me go if I told her the truth,* I reasoned. Mrs. Ryan gave me a look that could have knocked another gander down.

It was the end of October 1951 and it was time to boil the slops. My hands were bleeding as I had once again found broken glass; the urn was ready to empty of water, and I was getting angry at the saddleback. He was getting all the pieces I threw out with the water, so I thought of filling the bucket with the boiling water, and before I knew it, I had dumped it on his back. There was a squeal. He took off like a greyhound, around and around the field. *I must have scalded him* ran through my mind, and I was feeling ashamed of what I had just done in my anger. *Jasus, I shouldn't have done that.* Quickly I jumped down the platform.

I fed the pigs and cleaned the sties before getting on the horse and heading up to the field where I put him every evening to graze for the night. This night, as I approached the cottage of the little farm where the saddleback lived, I noticed a broom sticking out from the doorway, just a broom and a hand on it. I gave the horse a kick in the side, realizing that whoever owned that hand on the broom must have seen me scald their saddleback. Sure enough, she came out swinging the broom as I grabbed the horse's mane and slid over to distance myself from the broom, which beat down on the back of the horse just missing my head. The horse took off a full gallop, and I was hanging on for dear life, looking back at the confused woman in the middle of the road and not hearing what she was shouting at me.

I let the horse loose in the field, closed the gate, and walked home to my grandmother's wondering what I would do now. I told my grandmother that I was not feeling well and I'd quit the job. That weekend I asked my brother to go to Mrs. Ryan's and ask her for my wages as I was not very well myself to come over, and so ended my well-paying job.

"Messenger Boy Wanted," the sign in the window proclaimed up on William Street. I inquired inside. "Do you know how to ride a bike?" the owner, looking me up and down, wanted to know.

"I do indeed, sir."

"Do you know the streets around Limerick?"

"That I do very well, sir." I assured him.

"Well, I will give you a try. Come back in the morning at eight o'clock sharp."

I was delighted to tell everyone that I was going to be a messenger boy, with a bike supplied as well. I ran down to the Island Field to my Aunt Nora's, my face flushed as I proudly exclaimed my position pending the following morning.

She made a pot of tea from the dried-out tea leaves and gave me a scone, which she said she had baked. "Well Seanie, that is good news. Now save the money. Your mother has asked me to take you up to the garda station on Mary Street and get your travel identity card for England. She wrote to me just this week. We will have to go up O'Connell Street and have your picture taken first," she told me. "So can you meet me outside Cannock's Clock when you finish working?" She was laughing as she called to Uncle Mikey upstairs, "Seanie is coming with me to O'Connell Street tomorrow to get his picture taken for England."

I heard Uncle Mikey cough and hoarsely say, "Good luck, Seanie." He was very sick up in bed. Aunt Nora asked, "What time will you finish?"

"I don't know, Aunt Nora. Can I go run back?" I excitedly asked.

"When you finish your tea," she promised.

At which I gulped down the half cup of remaining tea and was out the door. I returned an hour later and informed Aunt Nora that I finished work at four o'clock, as it was Friday, and I made arrangements to meet her at Cannock's Clock that day. I cycled all over Limerick delivering little packets of groceries mostly to old people's houses, the basket in the front loaded with each delivery, and I was urging the day to hurry up and finish. At three o'clock I had finished my tasks, and the owner was very impressed, so he said, "Come back tomorrow again at eight o'clock," and told me to sweep up the shop and then go home when finished.

The next day I waited for Aunt Nora at the clock, excited at the thought of going to England to my mother. I had not seen her for over three years. But then I realized that I would be leaving my sisters and brother here in Limerick, and a bleak sadness came over me. I thought, *You are selfish, Seanie Morrisey. What about them?*

Aunt Nora came through the crowded street toward me. "Look at you, will you? You are tired looking, and your hair is all over," she said. She spit in her hand and brushed my hair down and spat several times to do so. "Fasten your coat."

"I have a rack in my pocket, Aunt Nora," I said as I reached into my pocket, and she took it and combed my hair.

"That's better," she said and told me to put the small tie on that she took out of her pocket. "That tie is Mikey's, and he has no use for it," she said, "so come on before the photo shop closes." Again, she spat on her hand, patting my hair down as we walked.

A week later it was November 6, 1951, as Aunt Nora and I went to the garda barracks, presenting the garda with the photo that was taken. The garda took it, stuck it in the travel identity card, and then stuck a stamp next to my picture and stamped it. "That will be a shilling, Mrs. Griffen," he said as he put out his hand.

Aunt Nora fidgeted in her coat pocket before finding the money. "Do you mind the pennies and halfpennies, as it is all I have?" she wanted to know.

"That will do," he replied, taking the change and counting it. "You are a penny short," he told her.

"Sorry sir," and again she put her hand back into the pocket and handed him a penny.

I was surprised to find our father at our grandmother's a week later. Perhaps word had got out that I had a travel card somehow, and maybe that was why he came back from England. He greeted me as I entered through the door. "Well, look at him now, Mother, all grown-up and ready for sailing the seven seas. Would you let me look at your travel card? You must have heard that I was coming to bring you to England with me," he said as I handed the card to him. "I have a good job for you in England, and your uncle Willy and Aunt Frances are looking forward to seeing you too."

I had not seen Uncle Willy since the time he gave me the shilling and I would not have known Aunt Frances, his wife, if she walked past me in the street. I was a little taken aback at this turn of events. *What about my mother?* I thought. *What will she think?* But she had not sent the fare yet, and I was anxious to go to England as soon as possible. So I resigned myself to going with my father.

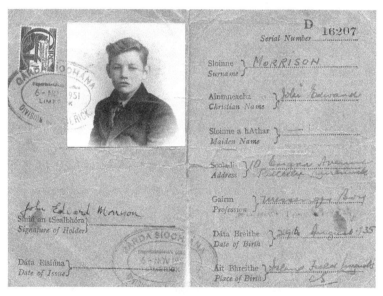

That cold November night on the ship, I woke from my recollections of the night my father had left us, to the ear-shattering blast from the ship's foghorn. My face was moist from the cold fog, and I looked across the deck to see my father leaning on the ship's rail. I got up, rubbed my tired eyes, and saw lights in the distance.

My father turned and said, "We will be in Hollyhead very soon, make sure your socks are tight." He'd had me put rashers (bacon packets) down my socks under the long pants that he'd bought for me in Limerick. I had tied string around the tops of the socks. He did not tell me why I was carrying rashers in my socks. "Just walk past the customs man and say nothing," he advised me as we approached the jetty in the late evening, the boat bumping as ropes were tossed to men on shore. I picked up my suitcase and followed my father to the gangway gate as the ship docked, and we waited in the crowd of other passengers to go ashore.

"A train will be waiting for us to take us to Manchester in England," he assured me. "We will be in Salford at your Uncle Willy's tonight and have some supper."

I walked through customs as he had told me and waited for him at the other side of the counter, alarmed to see him being led away into a room and out of my sight.

It was after about an hour that he came through the customs and saw me sitting by myself holding my suitcase. He did not say anything else after he told me to follow him to the station and I saw the train with the steam filling the station. It looked like the train that we'd left Limerick in, except it was red instead of green in colour, with English letters instead of Gaelic. The train hissed and jerked, wheels spinning on the steel track, and the journey started to Manchester as the night closed in.

A new chapter in my life was unfolding in a strange land. People spoke in a different tongue, very unlike what I had ever heard before.

The train rocked gently as we raced through the countryside. I was not tired and spent most of the journey with my nose glued to the window, not knowing what I was looking for, as my father slept opposite me. The train stopped several times at little railway stations, people getting on and some getting off. Finally, we came to a stop in Manchester. "Victoria Street," the sign said. We met my Uncle Willy on the platform, and he took my suitcase out of my hands. "Here," he said, "Seanie, let me carry your bags." And he gave me a hug and laughed as we left the station and walked through Manchester on our way to his home in Salford.

We passed a big prison he told me was Strangeways Prison, and a shiver went through my body. Uncle Willy brushed that aside by saying in the same breath, "What do you think of our grass here, Seanie? Not as green as it is in Ireland?" and I agreed as we crossed the road, passing a small patch of grass near a shop. My father was telling Uncle Willy that I had rashers in my socks. "Did you bring any nylons this time?" Uncle Willy asked. "There is a big demand for them here."

My father looked at him and said, "I will tell you later," as we walked down a small street to the house past houses that looked damaged from a war.

My Aunt Frances threw her arms around me and was crying as she looked me up and down. "You are very welcome, Seanie, to stay as long as you want, love," she said, giving my father a look that would bring a horse to his knees.

It was a short stay in Salford near Manchester. Just a week passed before my father informed me that we were going to Barrow-In-Furness, about ninety miles to the northwest. He said, "We will see what work we can get you at the shipyard Vickers-Armstrong's."

It was all double Dutch to me. I just nodded as we walked to the train station in the early morning rain. When we arrived at a train station called Dalton-In-Furness, he got up and told me we were there. "We will be going to a friend's house, and he is Mick Kavanagh," he told me. It sounded Irish. "Barrow is only three miles away," he continued as we walked the short distance, stopping in front of a police station where he told me he had saved a little girl's life when the police station caught fire. He explained how he'd climbed the downspout up to the window, kicking it in and bringing the little girl down again on his back. She had been trapped in the burning bedroom, which could not be reached from the stairs inside the station, he said. Her father was a policeman, and they lived in the station. I felt proud of him right then for the first time in my life.

Going up Stafford Street, we arrived at number 19, where we were greeted by Mr. Kavanagh and his daughter and her husband. "Well, Ned, this is Seanie," my father said as he presented me to the family.

They were very kind and told me, "You will be staying with us for a little while whilst your father gets you a job."

"How old are you, Seanie?" Ned asked.

"I'm sixteen and four months, sir," I informed him.

"Well, Seanie, you don't look it." He smiled as he handed me a mug of scalding tea and a cake. "There now, that will put some meat on those bones, Sonny."

"What are you thinking of doing with him?" he asked my father.

"I will take him to Barrow tomorrow, and we will have a look in the employment office."

We spent the night and the following morning caught the train to Barrow and arrived outside the employment office on Duke Street. Looking in the window of the office, my father saw there were several little cards with jobs posted on them. "Look, Seanie, they are looking for apprentices at the shipyard, electricians, boilermakers, coppersmiths, plumbers," he said.

But I did not have a clue what they all meant, so I just stared at the window as my father asked me what I wanted to do. "I don't know, sir."

"Dad," he corrected me.

"I don't know, Dad."

"Well, I will tell you that plumbing is the best. People have to eat, and people have to shit."

I was surprised to hear him swear. I was not used to that.

After receiving a note to go to the shipyard's office, my father said we would go right away, and we left the employment office. We stopped at a pub on the walk where we had a pork pie, and he had a pint of Guinness while I had an orange drink. At the shipyard, we were told to go upstairs to the office above the gatehouse and present the application to the officer there.

Sitting in the office, the officer asked my father what education I had. He looked at me, and I stared back at him with a puzzled look on my face. What did he want to know that for? I did not want anyone to know I had been in Glin for stealing and mooching from school. I said immediately before my father could answer him, "I attended Saint Joseph's school for boys in Ireland, sir."

"Do you have your leaving certificate?" he inquired.

"I don't, sir. I will send home to see if my grandmother can find it and send it to me," I lied.

I could see my father looking puzzled now; he'd left school himself at age eleven.

Producing a long three-or-four-page form, the officer was smiling. "Well, young lad, I will give you three-months' trial here in Vickers and see how you do. In the meantime, I want you and your father to sign this indenture paper, and we will need a witness."

My employer was my master, as stated in the indentures, and I a servant for five years.

We returned to the shipyard the following day, the form filled out, and we were accompanied by a friend of my father's as a witness to the signing of the indentures. The three of us left the office, and I was to start work the following morning as an apprentice plumber.

Before he had to leave to go to his job in another part of England, my father made arrangements for me to go into lodgings with Mr. and Mrs. Bowness in Barrow-In-Furness. He told me that I would be all right there. I could walk to work as it was not far, and Mr. and Mrs. Bowness would look after me until he came back again. Before he left the following morning, he told me my wages would be "thirty-two shillings and sixpence a week. For the bed and meals that are thirty shillings, she'll also make some sandwiches for your lunches, so that's grand," he said, tapping me on the head, and saying he would write to me.

I said good-bye to Mr. Kavanagh and his family, thanking them for their kindness to me for the week living with them, and I promised to come back to see them as often as I could.

This was a whole new world for me, and I tried to forget everything that had happened in Ireland. I failed miserably and would wake up at night in a sweat, looking around the little attic bedroom that I shared with three other men; Paddy, Jimmy, and an Englishman called George, who was in the little bed across from me. Paddy was almost deaf, and when we were downstairs he sat next to the radio and would have his ear almost glued to it as he listened to his favourite show, *Dan Dare, Pilot of the Future*. Jimmy was a labourer working on the roads and spent all his money on drink, and I rarely saw him as he left early and came in late. George was strange and did not speak much at all. When I watched him getting ready for bed, he would sit on his bed with his trilby hat on as he turned his back to me and slowly removed his pants, putting his pajama pants on. Next, he would take his coat off and put the top of his pajamas on over his shirt, take one arm out of the shirt, and put that pajama sleeve on, and the same with the other arm. He was then ready to go to bed, but he still had the hat on, which was the last thing to come off. The ritual was in reverse in the mornings; the hat was on his head first. It always brought a smile to my face and faces of the others.

There was a toilet downstairs at the next landing but it was off bounds to us in the attic except for the mornings when we could wash our faces. Mrs. B would hear the flush if you used the lav, so don't you dare. We had a bucket in the corner next to the one little window. Paddy took it upon himself to empty it out the window as it got half full of pee. There was the outside lavatory with newspaper-cut squares hanging on a string but no toilet seat.

I would babysit the landlady's baby daughter for a couple of shillings every week, and this also involved taking her to the live show about once a month. Before paying for the Russian steam bath, I would have two shillings and sixpence left from my wages that had a hole punched in it.

It was difficult to sleep in the little room, and I would wait with mistrust for all the others to be asleep before my eyelids closed. Glin had followed me across the Irish Sea, it seemed. No *clomp clomp clomp* of the wooden leg of the night watchman to give me assurance of peace of mind for that instant.

Just as I was falling asleep one night, movement from across the room startled me wide awake. *What is happening?* Again thoughts raced through my head, which was under the blanket, my heart pounding in anticipation of a frocked nightmare pulling it off me and checking my shaking, naked body again.

There was no sound of the swishing frocked brother's gown but there was the sound of the little window opening. I looked from under the blanket to see Paddy picking up the bucket, muttering to himself as he emptied it out the window.

There was an awful commotion in the back street as Paddy walked back to his bed, followed by a loud banging on the front door. "Jasus, Mary, and Holy Saint Joseph, in the name of God who would that be at this hour of the night?" Paddy muttered, pulling on his pants as we sat up on our beds. "The missus will throw a tantrum if it is Mick and he's full of the Guinness."

A howl from the hallway penetrated the attic. "Would you come down here? There's a policeman here drowned wet and stinking to the high heaven with a fag limping from his mouth, and he is not in a good mood. Come on down now, Paddy."

Paddy struggled down the dark stairs, and we could hear the shouting going on at the front door.

"What the f--- were you doing emptying piss out the window?"

"I didn't know you were standing under the window in the alley this hour of the night," Paddy replied.

"Well, that does not have anything to do with you!" the policeman shot back. "It is against the law to empty sewage into the street."

"But it is not sewage, it is only piss from the bucket, and it runs down the drain in the middle of the back alley."

The policeman chastised Paddy and told him that was the last time he would be warned, and he left. Paddy came back up the stairs, the missus telling him to look out the window in the future.

Paddy was mumbling as he climbed back into bed. "Having a crafty smoke while on duty, it serves him right. Piss on him," and he giggled as he pulled the blanket over his head. "He stunk of piss," he chuckled.

So the days passed swiftly for me, the evenings spent sitting around by Paddy's chair in the corner listening to *Dan Dare, Pilot of the Future* on the radio, Paddy's ear glued to the storyteller. Paddy's hearing was not very good, and the expressions on his face let you know how Dan was progressing in his fight against all odds. I was puzzled by the attention to a story of fiction, but Paddy liked it.

One day while I was at work in the shipyard at Vickers, one of the other apprentices, Walter, asked me if I wanted to go to the dance at the Johnny's on Friday evening. "What's the Johnny's?" I asked him.

"Saint John's Ambulance dance on the strand," he said.

"I don't know how to dance," I told him. "I never learned to do that."

"Well it's easy," he said. "You will learn in no time. I thought you Irish all knew how to dance, Johnny. Johnny Irish at the Johnny's." He laughed. We had become best friends.

I was getting used to being called "Johnny" now by the apprentices and Seanie was a hidden boy's past, buried in Ireland. I was terrified of being discovered as an Industrial inmate there a short time before. I would not have been able to handle that—they would disown me and make fun of me.

Friday came and Walter insisted that I go with him to the dance, which I did with some anticipation, as I had never been to a dance. That was the first time I set my eyes on a particular girl as I stood in the door of the dance hall, watching couples of my age dancing to the records playing loudly to their laughing.

I was watching Peg, who with Walter was gliding gracefully to the music. He had introduced me to her after we arrived. "This is Peggy," he said, and told her my name. I was still getting used to Johnny, but Johnny was to be dropped by my future wife, who I was about to fall in love with that evening at the St. John's Ambulance hall. This would be a bond to last our lifetime and beyond.

That evening as I strolled back to my lodgings, my head in the clouds, I was confused at my feelings for this girl. This was happening for the first time ever. An old Irish song stole its way into my heart as I thought of her; *She was lovely and fair as the rose in the summer, yet, it was not her beauty alone that won me, oh, no it was the truth in her eyes ever dawning, that made me love Peggy, the rose of Tralee.* "But she is from Barrow," I thought out loud and laughed to myself, *the rose of Barrow.*

The days seemed to take forever to arrive at each Friday when I could sit and gaze at the girl who had stolen my heart; Peggy Hancox, the paper-mill girl in Barrow-in-Furness, Lancashire. I was in a furness/furnace of my own, on fire and in love with this willowy, smiling, beautiful thief of my heart. Peg would spend the rest of her life with me and we would have three children; Michael, Karen, and Valerie.

One Friday I was in my usual seat at the Johnny's, when Peg came over to me and asked me to dance. I felt my face turn crimson and went into a panic at the thought of making a fool of myself with what I had learned from Walter and watching all the other dancers on the Fridays. The lessons that Walter had given me were about to be put to the test. She offered her outstretched hand towards me and I awkwardly took it to be led like a lamb to the slaughter. Holding her hand, I took the first steps into the dance to the 78 record on the turntable. I made several embarrassing fumbles in my old rubber-soled shoes on the polished floor, but she pretended not to notice. She was looking down on me, as I was not very tall at that time, possibly from the lack of sufficient food and nourishment whilst locked in St. Joseph's Industrial School. I was less than five feet tall, and Peg was a few inches taller.

"So you are Johnny Irish," she smiled.

A crimson flush again, not knowing how to answer, but "Irish" would stick with me for the rest of my life.

Going out with Peg soon followed as we both had fallen in love. She now liked going to the picture house on Fridays. Geez, I thought, my dancing was not "Fred Astaire." Maybe a better pair of shoes would have done the job. My wages as an apprentice just paid for my lodgings, except two shillings and sixpence, so Peg paid for the movies every week until I got a raise. And I started to grow taller as well, but one thing was for sure, even though taller than Peg, I would never look down on her.

Two years passed. My father had come to see me each year for a short visit as he was working around England. Peg and I decided to get engaged. We were just over eighteen years old, and I had saved eight pounds for the engagement ring. Then her mother and father asked me if I would like to live with them instead of in a lodging house. I fully agreed; her mam and dad were like my own parents to me. Peg's mother even gave me five shilling a week for pocket money.

In 1953 I was thinking that one day I would marry Peg. I told my father, for whom I had the greatest respect since getting to know him, that I wanted to marry her. He replied, "Not until you are a tradesman, son." I was disappointed but I respected his reply and would do as he said.

Regarding religion, Peg was a Protestant, so what was I, a Roman Catholic? I was not sure anymore, since getting released from Glin Industrial school. I wrote to the one Christian Brother who I trusted,

Brother Murphy, the man who had taught me to sing. His reply came back February 2, 1953. This is part of the letter.

You asked me a question, were you a Roman Catholic, yes John, you are, I can well understand why you asked that question because in England there is a branch of the Protestant church who call themselves Catholics. They have many ceremonies just like you would see in our church. They have a form of Mass but it is said in English. They even have a form of confession, they imitate us Catholics and many of them do become Catholics and great Catholics. Some of our famous cardinals were one time Protestants; Cardinal Newman, Cardinal Wiseman, I think, and several ministers have become priests. I would welcome any questions you would like me to answer. Write me again son I pray Jesus and our dear mother Mary, and your ever dear mother Mary to watch over you.

I am Dear John,

Yours Sincerely,

S. G Murphy.

My father came back to Barrow-in-Furness about once a year. One year he bought me my first suit; a ready-made suit, which cost eight pound, about twenty-four dollars at that time. He also wrote to me once or twice, letting me know where he was working. At the same time, my mother was also writing to me quite often and asking me to come visit her, but I was not getting time off work or enough wages to pay fares for travelling. I promised her that Peg and I would get there soon. She said she was working in a spinning mill in Bolton, Lancashire and was looking forward to us visiting.

With Peg's dad as a co-signer, I bought a motorcycle and paid for it weekly. So Peg and I we set off for Bolton, Lancashire to visit my mother at last. It was a very emotional visit and exciting. My mother wanted to bring Michael over from Ireland as well, which she did, and later on the girls came to visit as well.

We tried to get permission from the Catholic Church for Peg to become a Catholic. The time it would take was too long, though, as I was already called up for national service in the British Army; The King's Own Royal Regiment.

I finished my apprenticeship and the happiest day of my life arrived on December 1st 1956.

Peg and I were married in a registry office in Barrow-in Furness, Cumbria, which cost seven shillings and sixpence that day. She never became a Catholic but she was an angel with me for the rest of our lives and still is. Rest in Peace Peg. She passed away in my arms on January 20th 2016. It is still a terrible, heart-breaking situation for me.

We stayed at her mother and father's house, and we both worked; she at the paper mill and I at Vickers-Armstrong's shipbuilding and engineering for the next three months, waiting for the day I would have to leave, which arrived March 1957. Sadly, we parted, not knowing Peg was pregnant.

The train pulled out of the Barrow railway station, taking me to a new and exciting life with the little black suitcase that my mother had given me. When I was first called up, when they'd learned I was an Irishman, I was told did not have to serve the queen. I saw red at that statement; *Because I'm Irish I'm not good enough to serve?* I raised my voice and loudly told the recruiting sergeant, "If I'm good enough to live in your country then I'm good enough to fight for it."

"You have a temper, I like your balls, son," he said. "Come on in."

Peg and I, 1956/1/12

Three months of training followed before the PT instructor pulled me to the side one day and said, "You should apply for the SAS; Special Air Service."

"What's that?" I wanted to know.

"The pay is better, and you get to see the world," he replied.

I jumped at that offer, and he put my name in for the transfer to the SAS. Several weeks passed, and one day as I was in the armory, word came that I was accepted for the Special Force trials and to show up at Brecon, in Wales. This was the beginning of my introduction into active service in the jungles of Malay in the Far East. But first, I had to pass all the tests to belong to the finest special force in the world. There were to be three tests.

The train finally came to a stop on my journey to Brecon, a lovely little town in Wales. I stepped onto the platform with kitbag and suitcase, looking for whoever was to pick me up for transport to barracks somewhere in the village.

But an hour passed sitting on my own in the now-deserted station. Occasionally I stood and looked, and then finally, a couple of fatigue-clad soldiers approached. "Private Morrison," came the friendly inquiry.

"Sir," I responded, as I did not know what rank they were, but took no chances.

"Pick up your kit and follow us," and we went out of the station and stopped at the bottom of a steep hill directly outside. It was a warm day and I was dressed in full army issue. "If you go up the road," said one of the soldiers, pointing up the hill, "you will come to some gates. Report to the office, letting him know your name, rank, and number."

I let this sink in and before I realized that I was not getting into the jeep, they were gone. I looked in disbelief at the hill and then at my luggage, and threw the kitbag over my left shoulder. It weighed heavy, but I picked up the suitcase and started to climb the hill, sweating as I struggled with the awkward baggage. *Should have left the case at home,* I thought, as I finally reached the top of the climb. I looked for a gate or maybe an SAS sign, "SPECIAL AIR SERVICE REGIMENTAL BARRACKS," or a guardhouse manned by soldiers. There was no such sign or guardhouse on this road, but I spotted a gate finally at the end of the road. I saw nothing at all like a barracks but just a couple of what looked like long cabins with a jeep parked outside.

Inside the office I presented my papers to a soldier, no stripes or badges, just a fatigue outfit and a laidback attitude. He took my papers and pointing to a cabin told me to go find a bed there. I was glad for the end to this day and soon lay down thinking about what was ahead and wondering if I was the only one here. Later on I was joined by several others dropping their gear and taking their beds, one after another.

Weeks of strenuous testing in the mountains of Wales followed; assault courses, climbing, running, map reading, trig-point finding, shooting rifles and handguns, grenade throwing, while all the time all twenty-three of us attempting to become members of that elite SAS force were being vetted on our every move, our personalities, skills, and strength by Paddy N. and Mike J.

Finally we, what was left of the twenty-three starters, were interrogated in the office in Brecon in Wales. "What did you observe?" was the question as the location was pointed to on the map. "How many sheep were grazing?" And there were questions about our buddies' actions until we were dismissed to wait outside whilst Paddy and Mike, the only two in authority at this camp, discussed our futures in the regiment, if applicable.

Being called back into the office was one of the most terrifying moments in my life. Had I passed, or would I be returned to Unit RTU, from which I came?

"Well done, Morrison. Welcome to the first test of three and good luck to you."

Of the twenty-three hopefuls, seven passed this stage, and we were bound for Aldershot in preparation for the flight to Malaya where our parachute training would be in Changi. If we passed that, then it was back up to the base near Kuala Lumper and the final test of jungle operations. We were now down to six as one friend lost his nerve in the Ulu (jungle), and had to be clubbed when he pointed his rifle at the corporal. He was sent back to the UK, not in disgrace but with sympathy for coming so far and failing.

I recalled back to Brecon and Paddy N. telling me one day, there was word that an IRA (Irish Republican Army) operative had been reported in our area here in the village and might attempt to steal weapons from the armory. "I will put you in there for the night," he said. "If you hear anyone at the door, shoot. No one should be at the door."

I thought he was telling the truth and told him that I would. Thinking back, though, I realized that must have been another test; this one on my Irish background and my father's gun-running escapade with the flour barrels in Limerick. Paddy was a Dubliner, a great instructor, as was Mike, a great Welsh one.

That night, I was armed and reminded by Paddy that no one should be near the armory, and that if there was the slightest sound at the door to shoot right through it. I kept my rifle close to me all night, not closing my eyes, and was finally glad to see the first light the next morning.

So the stage was now set for action. Our next orders were to pack our kitbags and other belongings for our trip to the parachute-regiment base in Aldershot. The trip was by train. Arriving at the base, we were taken to our billets in the barracks, where we were issued bedding and clothing and advised that there would be an inspection of the clothing, which was to be washed, pressed, and squared and laid out on the bed in two days. I decided to locate a laundromat and do it there, throwing red gym shirts, shorts, etc. into the machine and starting it, proud of my smart move. The machine stopped and

I began collecting and filling my kitbag, but stopped, goggle-eyed, seeing with horror that all my whites were pink. Inspection came and I noticed the surprised look on the face of the young officer, who gave me a sideways glance as he moved on to the next bed. I was embarrassed and to this day pink is not my favourite colour.

This was a short stay at Aldershot Parachute Regiment base and we got our orders to get ready to move out for our flight to Malaya, which was a three-day trip with stops in Italy, Turkey, Pakistan, India, Thailand, and finally Singapore, where we were to undertake our parachute training of seven jumps from one thousand feet. There was also a water jump at five hundred feet into the South China Sea, dingies strapped to our backsides. A small oxygen bottle was attached, to open and inflate the little dingy, which had two paddles that strapped to your hands. You'd lie on your belly and paddle against the currents to be picked up by a speeding power boat.

Before the jump, as I shuffled with the others towards the door, watching for the green light from red over the doorway and waiting for a slap on the back to be told over the roar of the engines "GO!" the dispatcher said to me, "Morrison, you won't hear a splash when you hit the water, you will hear 'splash.'"

I gave him a look that would have felled an ox.

"It's full of Man "O" War jelly fish," he said with a grin.

After I jumped, hit the water, and went down several feet, maybe ten feet, my parachute buckle, which I had twisted and hit to release the parachute as I hit the water, nudged my leg. This caused me to surface at speed and to this day, I swear to God that I walked on water after the thought that a shark was about to have a chew on me. I was not worried about jelly fish.

On one jump, Tug Wilson told me that he was agnostic.

"You don't believe in God?" I said in disbelief.

"That's right," he replied.

"Why not?"

"I have never been in a church, I'm agnostic," he replied, as we stood to be dispatched.

As we shuffled to our stations, I was on the starboard side and he on the port side. Starboard side was to jump first. The little teddy bear with the chute on was thrown out to show the speed of the wind, which was considerable but not enough to cancel the jump. So I landed on the airport ground with no problem, and as usual I sat there waiting for the others to land, so as not to cause any problems for those still in the sky. It so happened that one jumper whizzed over my head at a fair clip and I heard him utter, "Oh God," as he hit the ground hard; Tug. I just gave him a knowing smile and started to unbuckle my harness and pick up my chute.

On another jump, the wind was fierce, so the pilot informed the dispatchers that he was returning to land the aircraft, but he discovered as we approached the airport, that the landing gear was not responding and would not bring the wheels down. He climbed back to one thousand feet and told us we had to get out. "Sorry guys." So we were dispatched into the gale-force wind, and we were hitting the ground pretty fast and rolling like balls. As we did, two men landed on the air hanger roofs; one went into a cement mixer, breaking his leg; and a few of us had aches and pains to follow. We sat down waiting to see how the plane, a Valetta, was going to land, seeing that the dispatchers and navigator had stayed on board with the pilot wrapped in their safety nets. They jettisoned the fuel and came in on the grass beside the runway. The plane flipped up on its nose, but all were safe.

Active service in the jungle came as a challenge to me, but I adapted to the task as a normal day's work. On my first day, I awoke and brushed a large, bird-eating spider off my face. It must have enjoyed my hot breath on its belly. Danger was not an issue with terrorists, but with leeches of various types; bull, tiger, etc. They were our worst enemies; their little bodies sitting on leaves, waving back and forth as we brushed past, hacking with our parangs (large, sword-like jungle knives) at the dense undergrowth on the trails. Looking at white scruff marks on the very large roots of trees, we tracked along trails that seemed recently used by, not animals but otherwise. Animals do not leave such marks in the chest-deep swamps, so these were indications of recent human movement through those paths.

Up in the trees, the terrorists would move through the deep tangle of brush and branches attempting not to leave any signs on the ground below. That is where the monkeys were our friends—what a racket they made when they were disturbed in their homes.

Being age twenty-three and ignorant of dying was a blessing; it never crossed my mind that I would die—I was invincible. Mind you, some little incidents tested my reasoning, like the time we basherd (set up camp) down on a buckit (a mountain) at around 2,500 feet, where we had settled down just off an elephant trail. This was not a good idea, and we should have known better as the trail across the mountain range was like a major highway—two lanes, mind you, nice to move on, head down-arse up, with a 110-pound Bergen rucksack on your bent back and wet through and through. The Bergen had all your two-week rations cuddling in it, and its straps cut into your shoulders. We got an air drop of rations about every two weeks in a three or four month operation.

We had to move out of the elephants' right of way that particular evening as they headed to their watering hole just below us, and we settled across the watering hole from their trampled tracks. We built hastily-made shelters of large attap (large leafs) and sticks. I, of course, was the loud snorer and the boys built their shacks a little distance from mine—great guys. I would visit and chat by candle-light with some of them, always making sure the rifle was almost glued to my arm. On one visit, I was chatting to Bill Hemmings and sitting on a protruding tree root, bare feet outstretched, with a hot cup of tea. The shelter's stick was stuck into the jungle floor with the candle flickering on top of it. Suddenly, I felt something sliding over my outstretched, crossed feet. I looked down, not moving a muscle, to see who the uninvited guest might be, but it was too dark under Bill's bamboo bed. I asked Bill to see if he could have a look, and he leaned over the other side of his bed and looked under. "Don't move Sean. He is still moving, must be a long bugger." Then the snake merrily went on his way into the lush undergrowth and into the night. "Quite a snake that one, Sean."

Going back to my shack and into my wet-dream sleeping bag, I woke in the very early morning to the ever-vibrant, trembling jungle, alive with the magical music of all the unseen creatures. I went for a piss behind where my head lay, and was surprised to find footprints of jungle-made footwear; footwear soles made in molds from the rubber trees in the jungle. My snoring must have scared the crap out of him/her, and my throat was quickly checked. "Lucky bugger, Morrison," Billy B said laughing.

"I will move next door to you next time," I warned him, with an evil grin on my face.

Billy sadly lost his life attempting to carry a wounded SAS comrade over his shoulders, (fireman-carry position) in Borneo some years later. The wounded comrade survived.

In the Malayan jungle of Far East Asia, our job was to fight a war, which was also called The Malayan Emergency, against the communist terrorists; CT for short, and their leader, Ah Hoi. It was a war which had begun in 1948 and we successfully completed it in 1959 when we sailed back to England, leaving some brave friends behind for their sacrifices. The trip home was a three-week cruise aboard a military ship.

Our job in that Emergency was to win the hearts and minds of the natives in the jungle to gain valuable information from them, and this we did.

Ah Hoi was a baby killer. We learned that when we came close to his lair in the jungle, a baby became unsettled and was about to cry. Ah Hoi reached across and strangled the infant in the mother's arms.

Ah Hoi and his army of terrorists surrendered to us. My service then continued in Europe before the East/West wall in Germany, before I returned home to civilian life in England.

THE JUNGLE

I often still think back to that time as if it was yesterday. I was twenty-three already, and the only jungle I'd ever known was a chestnut tree in the Island Field in Limerick, Ireland. We climbed those trees for conkers; the chestnuts. It was all the rage then to play with them. We punched a hole through the centre and pulled a string through, tied a knot, and after we had hardened them up the chimney, we challenged other boys to attempt to smash them with their conkers,. The trees in the jungle into which I parachuted and lowered myself to the jungle floor, had no chestnut conkers. They were 200-foot giants whose canopies blotted out the sun, leaving a steaming sauna and bountiful mosquitos, leeches, and ants, which were two-inches long, just to name a few. And then we had some not-very-nice ones that gave rise to the hornets, which were small-bird size. When we heard them approach it was customary to shout "Bandits!" and dive for cover.

Then there were things I had never in my life seen before. *How exciting*, I thought, *a walk in the park*. One day, sitting under a tree, as if I had a choice to sit under anything else, I lit one of my free-issue cigs from the customs people; seized contraband, they came in fifties in each tin. I lay back, striking a waterproof match, took a drag, and a cloud of smoke curled upwards toward the heavens somewhere above the canopy of the sunless, green blanket overhead. "Hey, WTF," I muttered as a stream of urine splashed onto my head. Looking up, I saw a chimp, proudly defending his jungle home from fire. *Clever buggers them chimps*, I thought. I swore he was smiling down at me. Needless to say, there was a soggy fag hanging from my lips, and Geordie, our radio signaller, had to try to contain himself from howling with laughter. After all, we were in terrorist country and silence was preferred if you wanted to enjoy this "walk in the park" for the foreseeable future along with our many wild-life bedfellows.

Eventually, word came by Morse code to Geordie, our signaller, which read, "Congratulations, Trooper Morrison. Son born 25th September."

Peg and I called him Michael after my father, because I had grown to love him.

SPECIAL FORCES

Interesting and funny incidents occurred. We had the Dayak warriors (head hunters) from Borneo as trackers with us and their sign of manhood was a headless tattoo on their windpipes. I had this tribal insignia tattoo done on my back, not my throat as I was not indoctrinated into manhood as a young Dayak is. The tattooing was done with two instruments made from bamboo. A sliver of bamboo served as the needle and it was tied with lalang (a very fine vine off of the tree) onto the end of a small-sized bamboo, which was to be the one that quivered or viBr.ated as it was struck. The small-sized bamboo with the needle was placed on a soft, raised cushion, in my case, my jungle jacket. Berries were used for the dye. The larger bamboo (the hammer) would strike the needle one, and it would quiver and vibrate as the recipient, me in this case, lay face down on the jungle floor. This was not before I had drunk a mess-tin cup full of G10 rum, which was dropped in our two-weekly, every so often, rations from the air. Lots of my warm blood trickled down from my back to the soldier ants, but of course it was painless. Just one interesting incident—there were many.

1960

My military service complete, getting back into civilian life was a little difficult for me. In April 1960, I returned to where I had left off in March 1957, back to my old job as a shipyard plumber and the boys who I had forgotten about; my workmates. Peggy was thrilled to have me home, and my son Michael wondered who I was, taking his place in the bed. I did not realize how the training and active service against CTs (communist terrorists) had affected me, (or was it my Glin experiences?) until one morning, Michael, my baby son, climbed on me in the bed as I was sleeping. My reaction was immediate. Jolting awake from a deep sleep, I threw my baby son into the air with all my strength, and he tumbled through the door and down the stairs onto the lower landing.

I could not forgive myself for that. My reaction shocked me, and thank God he was not harmed, though he cried a lot. I told Peg that I was terribly sorry and that I'd thought it was someone else attacking me. She understood and comforted me and Michael, who was only three years old and now scared of me. It took a long time to regain his trust.

Shipyard plumbing in Vicars Armstrong's shipbuilding and engineering in Barrow-in Furness, Lancashire was really pipefitting and had very little to do with plumbing at all . We worked on several kinds of vessels; aircraft carriers, a nuclear submarine, oil tankers, ocean liners, etc. and I even worked on the record-breaking speedboat, Bluebird, of Donald Campbell on Lake Coniston. I continued with this work for eight years before going into construction, travelling around England, Ireland, and Wales, working on oil refineries, cement plants, milk-marketing board projects, breweries, etc. etc.

We were blessed to have our baby daughter, Karen, join the family in November 1960, followed in 1965 by the daughter who would be the comedian: Valerie. One day, whilst working on an oil refinery in Grimsby, England, I saw an advert in the newspaper for pipefitters for a steel plant, Algoma Steel, in Sault St. Marie, Ontario, Canada. They offered good wages for tradesmen, transport to the country, and their family's fares as well. I applied and was accepted after passing some tests in Birmingham, England.

In April 1969, I was standing on Canadian soil and working at Algoma Steel—a dirty job, but I liked the change. I was settled with a French Canadian family of eight and another chapter in my journey began with the little black suitcase accompanying me. Three months passed at the steel plant and I sent for Peg and the children. I did not realise how much the move would hurt her and the children; she leaving her mother and father, who were like mother and father to me, and also the children leaving their friends. I should have known, for had it not happened to myself? Peg cried for months, day and night, so I thought that a visit home in what was called "the thousand dollar cure," (the reference is to the fares etc.) applied. This had been advised by some of the other lads, who had also experienced the same sort of pain for their wives.

Peg came back a much settled mother and the crying stopped. The children found new friends as well, only to be moving again shortly after, as the steel plant went on strike. I was offered support by the company to stay until the strike, which I was a part of now, ended. But I thought to myself what if that was known to the others? If I had taken that offer, I would have been lynched, so I started looking in the newspapers farther around the province of Ontario for other work. Mrs. Callahan, the landlady where we stayed in Sault Ste. Marie, had offered me a plot of land on St. Joseph's island. She had five plots and only four sons, and she said that plot would be mine. I thanked her for her kindness to us but said we had to move on for work elsewhere. This was my introduction into the fantastic kindness of Canadians.

As it happened, I and a few others who had come to Algoma from the UK saw that Windsor, Ontario was the best bet for work. I had bought an old car cheap, and we set off south for Windsor and a new beginning once again. We found a cheap lodging house whilst I and Peg looked for work. The children went to school, and I got a job for a company called Pony Express, driving at night to different towns around Windsor; my packages' contents unknown to me. I later learned that one such package contained over a million dollars. Peg found a job for an American company called Parking Devices and worked with an engineer, putting the electric components for automatic parking gates together. I studied at St. Clair college in the plumbing trade and finally at Lambton College in the steam-fitting trade as well as welding and was certified in the three trades. This took me into membership in the union of plumbers, steam-fitters, and welders and that helped us get our first new house in Windsor, Ontario.

My mother, who had kept writing to me, came to visit us and we had a wonderful time together for three weeks. During that time we took her to Long Island, NY to see her sister Mary, who she had not seen since she was six years old. However, when we arrived, Mary's daughter Kitty, who lived in Connecticut, informed us that Mary had died just three days earlier. We were devastated and my mother was heartbroken as we went to the fresh grave to pay our respects. It was a very difficult time.

We drove back to Windsor, Ontario after a couple of weeks with Mary's family; a very pleasant time. My mother's brother Tommy, whom she had also not seen since she was six years of age and who lived in New York, flew up with his wife to Detroit where we picked them up and you could not pry them apart for a couple of weeks. My mother was so happy, and so were Peg and I and the children.

I flew back to Limerick City, Ireland a couple of times to see my father for a few weeks, which were very pleasant as he was on his own. And finally I went back to bury him in the family grave. My mother had died in my arms in hospital in Bolton before that, when I flew back to visit her, and I buried her there.

It would be many years later that the abuse at Glin Industrial School and many others would be exposed. I was summoned to Dublin in and after the year 2005 to tell my story to an investigating board and I was compensated with a sum that I was told not to reveal or I'd be prosecuted for doing so. Following is more investigating that was carried out and published.

I extend thanks to the University of Limerick and to Thomas Wall, a friend who wrote *The Boy From Glin,* who furnished the university with all the documents made public, as he was the last inmate at Glin. He brought the abuses to light when he kept the documents even after he had been instructed to burn the evidence.

I was part of the investigation myself when summoned to Dublin from Canada to give evidence of my own experiences. The letter below was sent by my solicitors in Dublin in 2005.

Re: Commission to inquire into child abuse Investigation Committee Interview:

Dear Seanie,

I am writing to you further to previous correspondence with regard to the interview process, introduced by the commission to inquire into child abuse at the beginning of 2005.

I have recently received correspondence from the commission stating it intends scheduling you for interview sometime between 18th April 2006 and 10th of May 2006. The interview will take place in the offices of the commission to inquire into child abuse at Floor 2, St. Stephen's Green House, Dublin 2.

It is necessary for you to decide whether you wish to attend for interview before you are given a particular date and time for same. Consequently, please contact me by telephone to address any concerns or queries you have about the interview and I will be happy to discuss it with you in more detail.

If you do wish to participate in the interview process, you must make direct contact with a Witness Support Officer at the Commission to confirm same. This Witness Support Officer will then give you a specific date and time to attend and is available to make any necessary travel and accommodation arrangement for you. It is necessary for you to make contact with the Witness Support Officer before 5pm on 11th April 2006. The particular Witness Support Officer that you need to liaise with is. XXXX is contactable on 00 xxx x xxxxxxx.

Once again do not hesitate to contact me with any questions or queries you may have.

I attended the Investigation with my wife.

This investigation provided details of the abuse suffered at the hands of those who were our caretakers in the Industrial School in Glin. Some of their names are pseudonyms; their calling: Christian Brothers.

It gives readers facts about circumstances and events in the County Limerick, Ireland and beyond, which are burned into my memory. These facts are painful even today in my eighty-fourth year; it was a time that I will never forget. This then was the beginning of a varied life, which I will discuss in future writings, God willing.

I began my story sailing from Ireland at age sixteen and three months. This is where memories began to gather and ever since have sustained me. I look back, not in regret, but with some sadness at leaving my beloved country and childhood friends, and my brother and sisters.

It was starting life all over again, learning to live a normal life in strange lands; England and other countries, amongst strangers— poorly educated, undernourished, and wearing some of the clothes I was issued with on leaving St. Joseph's Industrial Institution or "school" as they called it at that particular time.

St. Joseph's is now demolished.

IT IS DIFFICULT TO FORGET THE PAST.

THE INVESTIGATION INTO CHILD ABUSE AT GLIN INDUSTRIAL SCHOOL.

The inquiry into St. Joseph's Industrial School, Glin, consisted of an analysis of the documentary material from various sources, namely the Christian Brothers, the Department of Education and Science, and the Bishop of Limerick.

The congregation supplied extra material between March 2007 and June 2008, pursuant to a decision to waive legal privilege that would, if it was applicable to the documents, have protected them from disclosure. Two reports on Glin gave information on the management and structure, and they have been used in compiling this report, particularly with respect to historical data and statistics. Mr. Bernard Dunleavy was asked to report on the archival material on Glin that was in Provincial House, Cluain Mhuire, and he asked brothers who had been in Glin to write memoirs of their experiences there.

Following this report, Br. John McCormack also researched the documentation and spoke to others who had been at Glin when it operated as an industrial school. The McCormack report was made available to the Committee in March 2007 and the Dunleavy report in June 2008.

St. Joseph's Industrial School began in a large, purpose-built block in Sexton Street, Limerick, in 1872. It was established under the Industrial Schools Act (Ireland), 1868, to care for and educate neglected, orphaned, and abandoned Roman Catholic boys, who were at risk of becoming delinquents and entering a life of crime. The underlying philosophy was that giving such boys a basic education and a trade would make them useful citizens by preparing them for work in industry or farming.

The school remained at the Limerick site until 1928, when it transferred to the former Glin District School in west County Limerick, where it continued until it closed in 1966.

THE MOVE TO GLIN

In 1894, Bishop Dwyer of Limerick proposed to the Local Government Board that children currently residing in workhouses of Counties Limerick and north Kerry should be gathered into a District School under the management of the Christian Brothers and the Sisters of Mercy. This District School was housed in the old workhouse buildings at Glin. In 1920, the school ceased to exist.

The Christian Brothers petitioned the Department of Education that St Joseph's Industrial School be transferred to this site from the now-overcrowded building in Sexton Street. The Minister for Education recommended the transfer to Glin, subject to a satisfactory report by the Inspector of Schools on the suitability of the buildings, and provided certain alterations and improvements were made to the existing buildings. Renovation and improvement works costing 15,000 pounds were carried out. They involved the installation of a new hot-water heating system, dining hall, infirmary, chapel, new floors in the dormitories, new windows and doors, new steam presses and new cookers.

In June 1928, the staff and boys of St Joseph's Industrial School moved to their new premises at Glin, some fifty kilometres from Limerick City. Despite the alterations, it was never a suitable building for a boys' residential school. A letter from the Brother Provincial on the 14th of November, 1961 suggested it did not become the property of the Christian Brothers. He wrote, "Glin was the only workhouse that was handed over to us and hence the only Industrial School for which we are paying rent to the Department of Health." Correspondence with the Christian Brothers confirmed that Glin never became the property of the Christian Brothers, but was leased at a yearly rent of forty pounds from Limerick Health Authority. In 1970, the premises were returned to the Authority.

The majority of boys who were committed to Glin through the courts came from impoverished and dysfunctional backgrounds. Some were committed for criminal offences. Court orders and school registers retained by the Christian Brothers show that, during the period 1940 to 1966, a total of 759 boys, of whom 131 were illegitimate, were committed to the school.

The number of children in Glin grew during the 1930s and 1940s, reaching a peak of 212 in 1949 and 1950. There was a steady decline in numbers during the 1950s and the 1960s, and the school was closed in 1966, at which stage there were forty-eight boys in residence. The following table sets out the numbers of boys in the school:

Year	Number under detention
1937	172
1938	154
1939	158
1940	158
1941	187
1942	200
1943	208
1944	200
1945	206
1946	208
1947	211
1948	211
1949	212
1950	212
1951	203
1952	187
1953	182
1954	190
1955	160
1956	142
1957	133
1958	123
1959	120
1960	103
1961	91
1962	90

1963	82
1964	80
1965	68
1966	48

The average age of boys committed to Glin was nine years and ten months, and the average stay of these boys was five years and eight months.

Mr. Dunleavy BL, in his report on Glin Industrial School, examined the reasons for boys being admitted. During the period 1940 to 1947, he tabulated his findings as follows:

Reason for admission	Number
Destitution	111
Larceny	62
Not attending school	61
Wandering	49
Having a parent not a proper guardian	38
Parents unable to control child	12
Receiving alms	10
Being under care of a parent with criminal habits	6
Homelessness	5
Fraudulent conversion	2
House breaking	2
Assault	2

Malicious damage	2
Total	362

His examination of the data revealed that, apart from one twelve-year-old boy who was sentenced for a period of one and a half years, "not one of the boys above was committed for less than the maximum period allowed by law." In short, no boy was to leave the school before the age of 16.

He went on to note:

> *Even if crimes such as larceny, truanting and house breaking, which may well have been motivated by poverty are excluded from the list of offences directly attributable to poverty—it is clear that over 48% of the boys were committed to Glin as a direct consequence of their impoverished backgrounds.*

Mr. Dunleavy stated that, between 1947 and 1966, the reasons for admissions were as follows:

Reason for admission	Number
Having a parent not a proper guardian	218
Destitution	95
Larceny	35
Not attending school	12
House breaking	7
Wandering	6

Homelessness	4
Parents unable to control child	3
Receiving Alms	2
Parent unable to support child	2
Fraud	1
Being under the care of a parent with criminal habits	1
Total	386

MANAGEMENT IN GLIN

The industrial Schools Act (Ireland), 1868 had envisaged that each school be under the control of a Manager and Management Committee, with the day-to-day running of the school under the supervision of a Resident Manager. In Glin, however, as in all Christian Brothers' industrial schools, the role of Resident Manager was assumed by the local Superior of the Community. The House Council, consisting of the Superior, Sub-Superior, and one or more Councillors, served as a form of Management Committee.

The numbers in the primary school in Glin varied from a maximum of 212 boys, in the late 1940s, to forty-eight when the School closed in 1966. The average number of teachers who served on the staff was five.

THE ROLE OF RESIDENT MANAGER

The Resident Manager was responsible for the overall management of Glin on a day-to-day basis. The duties of the Resident Manager included the health and welfare of the boys, admission and discharge, staff, management of buildings and property, and interaction with Government Departments and other agencies. He was also the Superior of the Community and Manager of the Primary School, the lay teachers, and the finance.

From 1936 until 1966, Glin had eight Resident Managers, three of whom served terms of six years.

Br. Jules was appointed Resident Manager in the early 1950s. He abolished the separate post of Disciplinarian and assumed the duties himself. In an internal Christian Brothers interview that he gave, he recalled in relation to discipline:

"There were no written rules. There was a general understanding of rules, passed on from year to year. I never saw the Rules and Regulations for the Industrial Schools."

Br. Coyan, speaking about his experiences in Glin, recalled Br. Jules and his attitude to corporal punishment in the school:

> "Well we had strict and firm orders from Br. Jules, he was the boss and the principal. We were not to punish a young fella, if any young fella became troublesome, he was to be sent to him. I remember that occasion when I had the run in with (a boy). It was reported to him and he met me the next morning and he ate me for dead and I said sorry I lost my temper and that's that."

In 1955, a Visitor remarked, "There is a homely spirit prevailing in our Glin Industrial School that could hardly be attained in a very large school." The post of Disciplinarian was never reinstated in Glin, and the subsequent Resident Manager in the late 1950s was considered kind and considerate towards the boys. A Visitor Report stated:

> "When the Superior came last summer a number of boys took to running away although they had been kindly treated. It appears that this phase is rather common at change of Superior. Now all have settled down again – The Superior is kind and considerate towards the boys and the boys respond well and seem to be quite happy and friendly. The Superior is not a believer in rigorous discipline."

Br. Hugues continued to be viewed as a successful Resident Manager in Glin and, in 1961, the Visitor reported that he was:

> a man of happy disposition, gentle, kind and self-sacrificing and not easily perturbed. He seems to possess the qualities which contribute to the efficient running of the school and happiness of the Brothers and boys.

The Visitor in 1962 remarked that the Superior was:

> Very highly appreciated by each and every member of the community for his evenness of disposition, his sense of fairness to the boys and to the Brothers…He is very kind to the boys and they appreciate this as shown by the good spirit in the place.

In 1964, the Visitor singled out Br. Hugues for his "efficiency, self-sacrifice, kindness to all and devotedness to duty…"

It would appear that from the early 1950s, the regime was less strict in Glin than in some other Christian Brothers' schools, and the influence of a kinder and more efficient Resident Manager had a lasting effect on the ethos of the school. However, the accommodation of the school in a former Victorian workhouse meant that what improvements were effected were offset by the unsuitability of the building for its purpose.

The personnel created the management system, and while that had the advantage of the system changing with the style and personality of the man assigned the role of Resident Manager, it also meant an inefficient Manager could seriously affect the working conditions and quality of life in the school.

Mr. Dunleavy, in his report on Glin, stated:

> *I encountered very little evidence of what one might term proper systems and methods in Glin Industrial School. There is no indication either in the archives or from the memoirs of Christian Brothers who formerly worked at Glin that any proper staff or community meetings were held in the school.*

He also added:

> *While the Brother Superior was ultimately obliged to take responsibility for the pupils at Glin, there is no evidence of any formal management structures at the school.*

FINANCE

In his report on Glin, Br. McCormack stated that from the mid-1960s the grant paid by the State was insufficient to meet the needs of the Institution. He concluded:

> *That this was the state of the school's finances in the last two years of its existence speaks volumes for the inadequacy of Government funding over the years.*

By 1963, numbers in Glin had fallen dramatically. In 1966 when it closed, there were only forty-eight boys in residence. Because State grants were paid on a per capita basis, a fall in numbers had an inevitable impact on finances, and the brothers were left with no alternative but to close down schools once they became uneconomical to run.

Throughout the 1940s and 1950s, however, numbers were sufficiently high to ensure an adequate income for the institution, and this was particularly so after 1944 when the State grants were made payable on the accommodation limit of the school rather than the certified limit. For Glin, this meant an increase of per-capita payments from 140 to 214. During this period, conditions for the boys in Glin were poor and reflected the funding that was available to the Institution.

The Visitation Reports for the period were not consistent in respect of financial information. The 1941 Report recorded a payment of 330 pounds to the Manager, 200 pounds to the Sub-Manager, and 120 pounds to each of the five other brothers working in the school. This represented approximately 25% of the State funding, which amounted to 5,014 pounds. It reflected a pattern seen in other Industrial Schools, where substantial sums were paid to the community account for the maintenance of brothers and of the congregation. The figures for 1940 were unusually high and there is no explanation as to why. Subsequent Visitation Reports recorded sums paid into the Building Fund and, by the time the school closed, it had 7,000 pounds invested in the Building Fund and a credit balance of 2,427 pounds in the bank. The sums invested in the Building Fund were "excess funds" from the institution.

PHYSICAL ABUSE

The basic stance of the Christian Brothers is that their institutions were not abusive and provided a positive experience for the boys who lived in them. They concede that, at certain times, some brothers may have overstepped the mark and used excessive corporal punishment, but in the main, they contend that rules and regulations were complied with.

The Christian Brothers also contend that, where serious breaches of the rules occurred, the matter was dealt with promptly and appropriately by the authorities.

There are eight cases, within the documentation provided, where excessive corporal punishment was used. Not all of the brothers mentioned below were working in Glin at the time the allegation against them was made. They are considered in detail below.

As in all the institutions run by the Christian Brothers, no punishment book was maintained. Without a written record of the nature of the punishment given, and the reasons for giving it, it is impossible to write about the extent of its use. The records that do exist are about clear excesses.

As set out in the General Chapter on the Christian Brothers, there were two sets of regulations governing the use of corporal punishment; the Department of Education regulations and the Rules and Acts of General Chapter.

With regard to the Rules and Acts of General Chapter, Mr. Dunleavy found that:

> *"none of the Brothers who wrote a memoir have any recollection of the existence of such rules." There were no written rules on the use of corporal punishment available to the Brothers within the school. They learnt how and when to punish from older, more experienced brothers, who told them or showed them what to do.*

By contrast, Br. Gaston, when interviewed by Br. McCormack for his report, stated,

> *"There was no written code of discipline, but all were familiar with the rules laid down in the Acts of Chapter*

and the injunctions of the Directory concerning punishment of pupils."

This informal approach to the regulation of corporal punishment increased the risk of abuses occurring.

This case concerned a boy, Paul Blake, who escaped from Glin following a severe punishment and went home to his mother. The story is recounted in a letter from a local councillor to the Minister for Education and the Minister for Justice:

It is my distasteful duty to draw your attention to what I consider is a matter of paramount public importance. [A boy's mother] called upon me on Wednesday last, the first instant together with her son... whom she stated was committed to Glin Industrial School. She further stated that the boy had escaped from the institution on the previous day, Tuesday 31st ultimo. She stated that he had received a flogging on Monday the 30th ultimo. She invited me to examine her son's back, which bore numerous dark stripes. There were also sores visible on the boy's back.

I issued a dispensary ticket to [a doctor] to have the youth examined at William Street Garda Station, Limerick, on the evening of Wednesday, the first instant, three days after the alleged flogging had taken place. He [the doctor] informed me that the boy's back bore evidence of having received a flogging.

On questioning the boy, prior to his agreeing to surrender himself to the garda authorities, he informed me that, as a result of his having not returned to the Industrial School at the end of the holiday period he was stripped of his clothes and flogged with a whip which had a number of leather thongs attached thereto.

Will you please state: If a form of punishment so described by this boy is prescribed by the law in certain cases in Industrial Schools and Borstal Institutions.

If the recipient of such treatment is compelled to be stripped or partly stripped of his clothing.

If it is compulsory for the Superior or other authorized person of an Industrial School or Borstal Institution to inflict such treatment in certain circumstances.

If the use of a whip with a number of leather thongs is prescribed and permitted.

If the report from Glin Industrial School agrees with the statement made to me by [the boy].

If it does not, in what respect does it differ?

I may mention in conclusion that on Wednesday night this boy who handed himself over to the garda authorities, later escaped form the members of the Glin Institution who had been sent to collect him at Limerick.

The councillor received an acknowledgment on 8th August. On 25th August he sent a copy of the medical report which read:

[Paul Blake] was examined by me at William St. Barracks on August 1st 1945. Examination revealed on posterior surface of right upper arm, on right forearm and on back – wheals – about 2 to 3" long. The wheals were not tender or sore and as such would be produced by a leather thong.

This medical report showed that Blake was severely beaten in a way that was against the regulations at the time.

Six weeks later, on 19th September, the councillor had not received a reply from the minister, so he wrote again.

> *"As this matter is now long outstanding I would like to have*
> *a full reply to my letter. Will you kindly facilitate me in the*
> *connection at your earliest convenience.*

The councillor was sent a brief note from the Secretary of the Department of Education dated 29th September 1945. The note said:

> *I am directed by the Minister for Education to say that he has*
> *had full enquiries made into the circumstances of the case and*
> *has taken the appropriate action in connection therewith.*

The councillor immediately wrote back on 1st October to demand answers to his questions, and to ask what "appropriate action" had been taken"

> *In view of the grave public importance of the case before us*
> *I would ask you to kindly answer the questions as enumer-*
> *ated in my communication of August 3rd. I would also want*
> *to be informed under what law and the date thereof that*
> *a youth could be submitted to punishment so described in*
> *my communication.*

This time he did receive a prompt reply, designed to put him in his place:

> *The Minister for Education desires me to inform you that he*
> *does not feel called upon to give you the information you have*
> *asked for in the matter unless he is supplied with evidence*
> *as to your right to obtain that information and is given an*
> *assurance as to the purpose for which it is required.*

The councillor asserted his right to be answered. He wrote:

> *My position as a public representative entitles me to the information requested – for the purpose of confirming the allegations made to me, which if correct should be ventilated in the interests of the public.*

He finally received a reply on 5th January 1946, but it was on condition that it should not be made known to anyone else. He inserted the following note into his file of correspondence:

> *Letter of 5th January 1946 withheld from this file as the contents were given to me at the direction of the Minister for Education for my confidential information.*

The letter has never been found.

On 15th April 1946 he wrote again to the minister. He asked for a general inquiry to be set up into the running of industrial schools, and for a specific inquiry into this case:

> *I am now fully convinced that nothing short of a sworn inquiry into this case will satisfy the public conscience, and I suggest to the Minister, that early steps be taken to set the necessary machinery in motion towards this end. I further suggest that the time is now opportune for an inquiry into the entire Industrial School and Borstal Institution system, and under these circumstances I would ask that consideration be given to extending this enquiry to cover every aspect of these institutions.*
>
> *I shall deem it my duty to lay the relevant information in my possession before a Tribunal set up by the Minister to inquire into the matters referred to herein.*

On 26th April he received a reply form the Secretary of the Department:

> *The Minister is satisfied that he is in possession of all the facts concerning the punishment inflicted, and in these circumstances he considers that a sworn inquiry as suggested by you is unnecessary and would serve no useful purpose.*
>
> *In regard to your further suggestion for an inquiry into the Industrial School system and the Borstal Institution system I am to point out that the Industrial and Reformatory School system was the subject of an exhaustive inquiry in the years 1934 to 1936 by a commission appointed by the Minister for Education. This report is now out of print, but you may be able to see a copy in a Public Library.*

On 9th May the councillor replied, giving vent to his anger at the secrecy about the case:

> *In my opinion, the useful purpose of an enquiry would be to put the public in the possession of the facts which the Minister and his officials and a few others only now possess.*
>
> *As the Minister refuses to give the necessary publicity, I am compelled to take other steps so that it may be procured.*
>
> *In your letter of the 5th of January you extended to me, under the direction of the Minister, an explanation for my confidential information. As the contents of this letter were conveyed to me in substance through other sources than that of the Minister, I feel that under the circumstances I would not be justified in withholding the information contained in this letter from the public or their representatives.*

The councillor wrote to the manager of the Theatre Royal in Dublin, who had contact with Fr Flanagan of Boys Town in the USA. He told him:

> *You have knowledge of this case, and I recall you saying to me some time ago, that you were approached by a prominent public man, who asked you to use your influence with me to drop this case. To your credit you used no such influence with me.*

The case, he said, was:

> *…this most degrading reflection on our system of detention of juveniles… These conditions will exist as long as Industrial Schools… remain closed boroughs to the public.*

He apparently handed all the documents, except the confidential letter sent on 5th January, to the manager of the Theatre Royal for forwarding to Fr. Flanagan. They were found in Fr. Flanagan's archives, and are the sole remaining record of the case. No record of this case was found in the files of the Department of Education.

While this correspondence was going on, there were other developments. On 12th October 1945, Paul Blake's mother received a letter saying:

> *The Minister for Education has informed me that he has granted the discharge of your son…Hoping he will be a success and give you complete satisfaction.*

Paul Blake was discharged, despite being still only fifteen. In 1946, the Resident Manager was transferred to Salthill, again as Resident Manager. Br. McCormack's research paper noted:

However it is also open to the interpretation that, following the publicity of October 1946, during Fr. Flanagan's visit to Ireland, the Provincial was using the first available opportunity to remove Br. Delaine from Glin. This would have been at the New Year, a time when changes were common and would not attract gossip.

Commenting on this case in a recent communication the Christian Brothers wrote:

Without contemporary evidence other than the (the councillor) Department correspondence it is difficult to piece together the full story of this incident. There is no doubt that a serious breach of regulations did take place but the identity of the brother mentioned in the account of the beating is not clear. The account mentions the "Head Bother," but since no name is given…boys in industrial schools could confuse the functions of responsible staff such as Resident Manager (a rather aloof figure), the Disciplinarian, who was in charge of general discipline, and the Principal, who was in charge of the primary school and classroom discipline.

FATHER FLANAGAN'S INTERVENTION

Father Flanagan made no mention of the Blake case while he was in Ireland, although his attacks against the punishment regime in Irish penal Institutions received widespread publicity. In a public lecture in Cork's Savoy Cinema he told his audience, "You are the people who permit your children and the children of your communities to go into these Institutions of punishment. You can do something about it." He called Ireland's penal institutions "a disgrace to the nation" and then issued a public statement saying, "I do not believe that a child can be reformed by lock and key and bars, or that fear can ever develop a child's character." His resolute and vociferous stand against the corporal punishment of children led him to speak out against the Glin case when he received a letter from one of his contacts in Ireland, Walter Mahon Smith. It stated, "As regards the Glin case, none of the daily papers would investigate or publish this for me."

When he got back to America, Father Flanagan spoke about it to the American Press. The matter was raised in the Dail in debate on 23rd July 1946.

> *Mr. Sean Brady TD asked the Minister for Justice, Mr. Boland:*
>
> *Whether his attention has been drawn to the criticisms of the prison and Borstal systems in this country reported to have been made by Monsignor Flanagan during his recent visit and published in the Irish newspapers, and to similar criticisms made on his return to the United States which were published in the New York press on the 17th July 1946, and whether he has any statement to make.*

Mr. Boland replied:

> *My attention has been drawn to the criticisms referred to. During his recent stay in this country Monsignor Flanagan did not see and did not ask to see any of the prisons or the Borstal institutions. I am surprised that in these circumstances an ecclesiastic of his standing should have thought it proper to describe in such offensive and intemperate language conditions about which he has no firsthand knowledge.*

Mr. Flanagan TD asked if the minister was:

> ...*aware of the fact that Monsignor Flanagan did not make these statements without very good foundation and very good reason for them.*

Mr. Brady TD asked,

> *if his attention has been drawn to a statement made by Monsignor Flanagan and published in the American Press, that physical punishment, including the cat o' nines tails, the rod, and the fist, is used in reform schools both here and in Northern Ireland.*

The Minister replied:

> *I have a cutting from a paper which contains a statement to that effect. I was not disposed to take any notice of what Monsignor Flanagan said while he was in this country, because his statements were so exaggerated that I did not think people would attach any importance to them. When, however, on his return to America he continues to make use of statements of this kind, I feel it is time that somebody should reply...*

After an interruption, he continued:

> *All I have got to say is that these schools are under the management of religious orders, who are self-effacing people, and who do not require any commendation from me.*

The Minister chose to attack the man who had attacked the system. His support for the religious orders closed the debate.

Brother Serge

Brother Serge was sent to Glin in the mid-1940s and spent two years in total there, with a break in service to complete his teacher training. A letter was apparently sent to Dr. McCabe, the Medical Inspector of Industrial Schools, complaining about the punishments Brother Serge had inflicted on the boys. The Visitation Report of May 1947 goes into the affair in some detail. The Visitor wrote:

> *For some time back certain members of the Limerick Corporation have been seeking interviews with boys from the school to provide information for certain members of the Dail whose ambition seem to be the providing of trouble for the government. The reaction of the situation on the boys of the school gave serious trouble to the brothers in the execution of their duty. A letter was sent to Dr. McCabe, medical inspector of Industrial Schools, giving information on punishments inflicted on some of the boys recently. She came along and held an inquiry which was strictly confined to the boys; she interviewed no member of the staff in connection with the matter. It is the unbiased opinion of three senior members of the community that from the information they got from boys interviewed by Dr. McCabe the information supplied to her in the above letter was substantially true. The brother implicated in these charges was Brother Serge, who is due to make Final Vows next Christmas. His method of punishment as far as I can make out, varied, once at least, from the recognized use of the strap. He had no discretion as to the number of slaps that should be apportioned to offences. Br. Serge has also been charged with acting as the leader of the troubles in the Training College towards the close of last year. I have met several brothers who were there at the time and all are agreed as to his guilt… I would not resent Dr. McCabe's attitude*

because if she succeeds in securing information from the boys,
the work of the politicians will be short circuited and danger
of publicity eliminated.

The letter of complaint to Dr. McCabe has not been discovered. Nor is there a report on her visit to the school, even though her interviews with the boys apparently uncovered allegations of serious physical abuse.

The Visitation Report cited above made several criticisms of a serious nature. It alleged, first, that Br. Serge had punished "some of the boys" excessively. Second, it alleged that Br. Serge could give an excessive number of slaps, and he could do so even if the offence did not merit a severe punishment. Thirdly, it alleged his method of punishment "varied once at least from the recognized use of the strap." The recognized use was usually a slap on the hand with a leather and, clearly, Br. Serge had departed from these guidelines.

The Visitor sent his report to the Provincial, who responded that:

It is a pity that the school has not a better reputation for
kindness and consideration for the poor boys. Nothing should
be left undone to secure kinder treatment of the boys and a
happier and brighter feeling among them. This is not only
possible but easy to secure if the brothers have the correct
feeling for them.

This reply was significant. The Provincial regretted that the school had not a better reputation "for kindness and consideration" for the boys in its care. He not only criticized Br. Serge, but all the brothers for not having "the correct feeling" for the children. This expressed unease about how boys in general were treated at Glin.

Five brothers referred to Br. Serge in internal Christian Brothers interviews. Their comments on him were illuminating. One Brother,

(Br. Coyan) who went to Glin in the early 1950s and who was clearly referring to Br. Serge, said:

> *...there was one there before I went there and he was very cruel. He left the brothers. There was a big inquisition from either the Department or the Health Board—his name won't come to me just now. He was sent out of Glin and the kids were complaining about him continually and you daren't mention his name. They hated the thought of him but he was sent down to the brothers and he was sent down to the place but we followed his career afterwards. He became a principal outside and a parish priest was in trouble, but that's the only case and that was before my time.*

He then added:

> *I have often heard it from the lads themselves about this man. He could be dead by now for all I know, he was a bastard as they say and the kids hated the sight of him and he was a man who should never have been sent to Glin. To be sent to a place like that you have to have great rapport with the kids like. You are living with them as much as you would if you were in a family at home and you have to coax them along... You are the only one that they can rely on...*

Brother Hardouin, who was in Glin in the 1940s, also recalled the man:

> *I can recall when the Department Inspector called to Glin to investigate a complaint made by a retired brother against a member of the teaching staff who was accused of being too severe. The brother accused was removed to a day school and the following Christmas was expelled from the order. I imagine that the complaint may have been a contributory*

factor in his expulsion although he had previous problems during second-year training.

Br. Zacharie, who replaced Br. Serge, said:

I came there from Monaghan to replace a brother who had been moved out because he was over severe... I was advised to be nice to the kids and not to worry about examination results.

Br. Gaston, who was resident in Glin during the 1950s, recalled talk about this brother being investigated. He said:

I cannot recall any situation where a formal complaint against the school was investigated by an outside group or individual, though I believe that there was such a situation in the school within three or four years prior to my coming.

A contemporary of Br. Serge, Br. Amaury gave more details:

The procedure for dealing with complaints would be that if any staff member or child in the school had a complaint he could bring that problem to the Superior/Manager, the sub superior, the school principal, the disciplinarian, or to the provincial or any one of his council. One such complaint was made during my year in Glin. It was made against one of the brothers on the school staff. I do not know to what outside group or individual the complaint was made but the nature of it was that the man in question was over severe in having recourse to corporal punishment. None of the details of this complaint were made available to the community or staff in Glin. The boy who was named as the one who made the complaint was personally known to me and my impression of him was that he was a boy who would be very unlikely to do anything serious enough to merit severe corporal punishment. He was known to have been a close friend – a "master's pet" – of one of the men who regularly did supervision in the school yard during recreation time. This does add more than a little likelihood to an opinion circulating at the time; that it was the "master" and not really the "pet" who caused the complaint to be made.

There are no grounds to suggest these recollections are unreliable. They all recall similar details and they provide an important illustration of how a violent man was dealt with by the management of the congregation in the 1940s.

First, there did not seem to be a standard reporting procedure for either boys or brothers when violent or abusive behavior did occur. Br. Hardoulin summed up the situation as he saw it:

Generally speaking there was no redress for any child who had a complaint against a staff member. Again as a younger brother, I certainly was not fully informed of problems that were the responsibility of management.

The procedure referred to by Br. Amaury, "that if any staff member or child in the school had a complaint he could bring that problem to the Superior/Manager, the Sub-superior, the school principal, the disciplinarian, or to the Provincial or any one of his council," was not used in this case of extreme violence. Instead, a letter of complaint was sent to an outsider; the School Inspector. There was no explanation in the documentation as to why this route was taken, but it was clearly deemed necessary or politic to avoid the congregation's management structures.

Br. Serge was removed promptly during the Visitation, and was sent to a day school. Some of the brothers in Glin informally kept an eye on his later career. As stated above, one of them believed that he had got into trouble elsewhere. He said, "we followed his career afterwards, he became a principal outside and a parish priest was in trouble," but no details are available about such an episode.

Given the seriousness of his behavior and the excessive violence he was known to have used, this simple expedient of removing him to a day school could not have guaranteed the protection of other children. Br. Serge's career continued as a national school teacher in a number of schools. He left the Christian Brothers in the late 1940s. He subsequently spent many years as a principal of a national school.

Brother Amaury

Brother Amaury worked in St Joseph's School for Deaf Boys, Cabra before moving to Glin where he spent a year during the 1940s. He made a bad impression during his brief period in Glin. During an annual Visitation, the Visitor was very critical of Br. Amaury and recommended his transfer. Br. Amaury was moved a few months later to a day school and did not teach in a residential school again. The Visitor made insightful observations on the vulnerability of boys in residential care:

> *With the exception of Br. Amaury all the other members of staff are capable and reliable. In punishing boys he sometimes loses control of himself. I would recommend his change in view of circumstances in the school. It would be better if Br. Amaury was sent to a day school where boys would have a parent or relative to interpose between themselves and a cruel teacher. The industrial school boy has no redress but suffer on.*

Perhaps due to the fact that two brothers in one year were accused of excessive violence, there is evidence that Br. Jules, who subsequently became Resident Manager, made efforts to change attitudes in the school. But it is not clear if he was able to eliminate abuses by brothers during his period of management. Br. Coyan, who was there at that time, remembered the rules laid down by him.

Brother Jesper

Brother Jesper spent over eleven years in Glin from the late 1940s. He held the position of councillor for his first seven years, before taking over as Sub-Superior in the mid- 1950s. The Visitation Reports reveal that he could be a difficult person to get along with and he was acknowledged as being odd. The Visitor noted that relations between him and a number of brothers were bad and, when questioned on the matter, his colleagues accused him of having a very bad temper. The Visitor subsequently remarked that Br. Jesper was "not quite normal." He was suspicious and aloof. By the late 1950s, his doctors recommended that he be transferred from Glin immediately, because he was in danger of having a nervous breakdown if he had to stay there.

There were reservations about Br. Jesper from his early days in the congregation. The Superior General wrote to him in the mid-1930s and drew his attention to a trait that cast doubt on his suitability to take perpetual vows. He reprimanded him for being:

> *Altogether too strict and harsh in your dealings with your pupils. It would appear that you are subject to moods, being at the one time rather depressed and gloomy and at others jubilant and vivacious… Possibly in class these variations are manifested by a want of uniformity in your dealings with the boys, treating them indulgently at one time and again with great severity…Harshness towards pupils is out of date. A good educator is never severe towards those he is training. Severity alienates the sympathy of the pupils with their teacher and loses to him their cooperation, the most powerful means he has for success.*

Nevertheless, Br. Jesper took his final vows shortly after this reprimand.

Br. Jesper completed an internal Christian Brothers' questionnaire in 2001 regarding life in Glin. He stated that there was "strong discipline" in the school but that it was not as tough as discipline in day schools. "It certainly was not hard." He denied that the boys were beaten regularly and "it would have been an exception arising out of a grave infringement of the rules that they would be in any way chastised." He conceded that the leather was used, but asserted that he had dispensed with its use shortly after his arrival in Glin. He denied any allegations of physical abuse made against him, and indicated that he would be surprised if similar allegations against his colleagues were true.

Brother Jeannot

Brother Jeannot was sent to Glin as a young brother in the late 1940s, and he remained for more than five years. In the early 1950s, the mother of two boys resident in Glin made a complaint regarding severe punishments her sons had received at the hands of Br. Jeannot. There was no proper investigation.

The two brothers had been committed to Glin a number of years previously, following the separation of their parents. The older of the two, described by the Superior as "a big hefty fellow," was regarded as troublesome. On one occasion when his mother came to visit, he complained to her that he had been punished excessively by Br. Jeannot. He alleged that he had been beaten with a stick and kicked by him. The mother demanded that her boys be released into her care, alleging that both had been ill-treated by Br. Jeannot. The Superior explained to her that the Minister for Education would have to make an order for their release. She then wrote to the Superior General, perhaps thinking that he could direct the releases, and the Provincial Council therefore became aware of the matter.

The Provincial wrote to the Superior of Glin, seeking information on the incident.

The superior responded by letter and explained that one evening, Br. Jeannot was in charge and reprimanded the boy for misconduct but he still continued to be impertinent. Br. Jeannot then called him into the play hall and struck him on the cheek before administering the leather. The Superior was convinced, as a result of his investigation, that Br. Jeannot had not beaten the boy with a stick or kicked him. He was also satisfied that the younger brother of the boy had never been punished by Br. Jeannot. He chastised Br. Jeannot for not bringing the boy to him to be dealt with. The Superior was suspicious that the mother had exaggerated the incident so that she could secure the release of her sons. The Provincial was satisfied, as a result of the information provided by the Superior of Glin, that "it is quite clear the chief difficulty in the case concerns the home circumstances of the children. It is well however that the brothers gave no serious reason for complaint in connection with their treatment of the boy."

It would appear that he reached this conclusion without the parents or boys being interviewed, and was quite happy to accept at face value the version proffered by Br. Jeannot and the Superior.

COMPLAINT BY MR. DUBOIS, NIGHT WATCHMAN

Mr. Dubois was employed as a night watchman in Glin in the early 1950s. He held the position for six months and stated that he left for health reasons. He wrote to the Department of Education shortly after leaving Glin, setting out a number of serious concerns he had for the boys resident there:

Dear Sir,

May I respectfully direct your kind attention "in confidence" to the following and I am confident that by doing so that I shall be doing a great work of charity.

For the past six months, I was employed as "night-watch man" at St Joseph's Industrial School Glin Co Limerick, and having had close contact with the "Boys" and with the running of the school in general, I am in the position to be able to make the enclosed observations and respectfully request that the Inspectors of this department see after the matter and do their best to remedy the state of affairs existing there.

The Boys are discontented with the existing state of things due to the following defects.

Poor food and clothing. The cook in Boys Kitchen has no knowledge of cooking being an ex-pupil working for 15 shillings-per week and has never got any training for this work.

Everyone employed at this school are free to have a smack at the Boys including the Brothers who appear to be indifferent to all this. The Boys' beds and sleeping quarters are very poor and during the cold winter months are never heated, neither do the Boys get any kind of winter clothing to keep them warm. The Boys shirts are very poor quality and very badly washed the whole place and system is very-very bad.

The Infirmary is just the same. The nurse goes off duty pretty often and the children are left to the mercy of one of the boys. I know the Brothers can scrape out of any difficulty but I write from personal experience, and if you could arrange surprise visits night and day, you could see for yourself. I could never have believed that such could exist in a Catholic Country. I know there is a good deal of window dressing to deceive the eye of the visiting official but I learn that the Boys are warned not to complain. May God help the poor children.

There are only two tradesmen in this school, a shoe maker and a tailor, no carpenter employed. How can we expect such Boys to become an asset to the state? They shall treat the state as the state treats them. Pay a surprise visit to this school some cold night and see for yourself. The former night watchman, a common farm labourer, carried a heavy leather when on duty and beat up the poor children as he pleased. Please Sir, remedy this and you will have the blessing of God and the prayers of the poor children. God bless you.

Yours respectfully

Mr. Dubois

In confidence.

The inspector of Industrial and Reformatory Schools, Mr. Sugrue, requested Dr. Anna McCabe to investigate the serious complaints contained in the letter, which he specified as food, clothing, bedding, laundering of clothes, and heating of the school in winter. Dr. McCabe visited Glin for this purpose, and she also took the opportunity to carry out a General Inspection. Her brief report on the complaints stated:

Mr. Sugrue,

I visited Glin Industrial School and had a long talk with the Manager. I told him about the letter we had received and which it was my duty to investigate.

I really could find no ground for complaint in the school. It is well run and the boys appear well and happy.

I asked the manager if there could be any spiteful reason why the letter should have been written and he told me that the man had been dismissed for insubordination and had vowed to injure the school... Apparently he thought that writing this note he would cast reflection on the school.

Many improvements have been made in this school and in my opinion there are no grounds for complaint against the management.

Given the very specific complaints made in the letter, this investigation was cursory and the report vague and unsatisfactory.

Dr. McCabe's visit was not only to investigate the complaint. She carried out a General Inspection on the same day, and her report gave little indication of the serious problems that she was investigating, and which were acknowledged by her superiors in the Department as needing special investigation.

Mr. Dubois then wrote a letter to the Minister for Justice, elaborating on the contents of his letter to the Department of Education:

Dear Sir,

May I respectfully direct your kind attention "in confidence" to the following hoping that you Sir will do something to help the poor unfortunate children concerned.

For a period of six months, I took up a position of night watchman in one of our Industrial Schools "for Boys" namely St. Joseph's School Glin Co Limerick and I may tell you Sir, that I never expected to find in a Catholic Country like ours, the awful bad conditions in so far as the poor Boys were concerned, only that I had spent six months and seen for myself I never could have believed that such conditions could exist especially as this Institution is under the care of our Irish Christian Brothers who are so reputed for teaching etc.

When I took up employment there last March, I found the poor children in a very nervous state, due to harsh treatment at the hands of the former night man (a local labourer) rough and cruel, who was allowed a free hand to beat up the children as he pleased, and was permitted to carry a heavy leather for this purpose. The children were called out of their sleep every hour to use the W.C and any poor child who had the misfortune to wet his bed, was very roughly treated by this night-man, who also reported the matter to the Brothers in the morning, and a further punishment was then administered to the poor child by the Brothers concerned. The children have no redress whatsoever and are just like convicts.

With regards the food it's very-very poor and the person in charge of the cooking is a young boy aged about 17 years an ex-pupil of the school, who at the age of 16 years was discharged, and sent to a job... but did not get on well and was sent back to the school, and the Superior... appointed him boys cook, but he knows nothing whatever about cooking and what he cooks for the poor children isn't fit for pigs to eat and I often felt sorry for the poor children especially the young and helpless ones. The Children get very little butter, their bread is served almost dry, they are allowed 2 slices of bread each with a little scraping of butter or marg, and an extra slice dry. The tea or cocoa is very light and badly made. The Brother who is supposed to supervise the Kitchen, Br. Warrane never bothers to do so, as he is a jack of all trades and never has much time to look after any job properly apart from the motor car which he drives. This Br. Warrane is a sour kind of person and never speaks a kind word to any of the children, and is very severe with the leather which he is very fond of using. All the employees are allowed to beat the children especially the plough-man (Mr. Prewitt) is very hard on the children working on the farm and very fond of using the boot, and his fist.

The children are very badly clothed. They are not supplied with any winter under clothing, neither are the sleeping quarters heated in winter and the poor children told me that they felt very cold at night and if they complained the Brothers would only laugh at them. I have experienced some cold nights at the school and what must it be in the winter! I respectfully beg to hope Sir that you will look into the matter. I sent a confidential report to the Dept. of Education but not enough to cover all I have observed during my six months at the School. The Infirmary part of the school needs overhaul and the present nurse is very fond of being away as she is local. She appears to have no love or sympathy for the children and the children will suffer much before they report sick as they don't like the nurse. In my humble opinion Sir, the whole school needs a good honest overhaul and a few night surprise visits. There appears to be a good deal of window dressing and outward appearances. No one has seen the meals served out to the poor children but I have Sir and all I have to say Sir, is may God help the poor little ones, they are a pity.

The position of night man in such schools is a very important one, and I respectfully suggest Sir that you should interest yourself in the type of person employed, and draw up rules and regulations to fit the job. The children are at the mercy of the night man during the night and it's important that such a man should be a sober man and have patience and charity in his dealings with the children, and Glin School can tell some queer tales about night-men. One thing I found most lacking in St. Joseph' Glin was charity. The only place I've seen real charity was with the Good Brothers of St. John of God in St. Augustine's Blackrock Dublin, and what a pity *these fine men cannot have charge of our Industrial Schools for they have at heart the real love of God, and in the poor children they see Christ Himself.*

I feel now Sir, that I can feel at ease as I was worried when I had to leave the children as my health would not permit me to continue the work, as I never smoke or drink I suited the job and I had the full confidence of the boys, who regretted my leaving and I promised them I would look after their interests. Do your best Sir, and look out for window dressing and bear in mind that the children are afraid to complain to any visiting official and you cannot expect much help from them.

God bless you Sir,

Your obedient Servant

Mr. Dubois

Confidently

The Minister for Justice wrote to the Minister for Education commenting that Mr. Dubois appeared to be an intelligent, well-meaning person and, if what he said was true, it revealed a very serious state of affairs. He asked to be kept informed of the results of any investigation.

Mr. Sugrue of the Department of Education visited Glin and wrote a memorandum in Irish recording what happened. A translation is as follows:

GLIN SCHOOL

I visited this school... and had a long conversation with the Resident Manager about the complaint made by Mr. Dubois in relation to school matters. I read the letters written by Mr. Dubois to certain boys in the school, to a maid in the school, and to men employed in the school. The Resident Manager had all these letters. According to the letters, it would appear that Mr. Dubois took a keen interest in the care of the boys at the school in the matter of food, clothes, etc. The Resident Manager told me that Mr. Dubois was wont to come downstairs at night and carry bread from the Brothers' refectory to the boys in the dormitories. From their appearance it would seem that the school shows great kindness and consideration to the boys.

Despite the fact that Mr. Sugrue had previously drawn Dr. McCabe's attention to the specifics of the complaints made in Mr. Dubois' letter to the Department of Education, and that more detail had been furnished in the letter to the Department of Justice that preceded his visit to the school, no detail is provided as to the quality of care given to the boys.

When a reminder was sent from the Minister's secretary, asking whether a report was yet available, the matter was taken in hand by a senior official, who reported to the Secretary of the Department:

Runai,

Glin Industrial School.

Complaint from Mr. Dubois, ex-night watchman there, to Minister and to Minister for Justice, re treatment of boys.

The charges made by Mr. Dubois may be listed as follows:-

- *The boys are poorly clothed, and have no winter underwear.*

- *The food is meager, poor and badly cooked.*

- *The sleeping quarters are ill-equipped and unheated.*

- *Employees are permitted to beat the children with straps and even to strike and kick them and to treat them otherwise cruelly, and even some of the Brothers are careless or unkind or given to beating the children with small cause.*

Dr. McCabe and Mr. O Sichfhradha have both visited the school and their findings, herewith, may be summed up thus:

The facts reported under charges (1), (2) and (3) are true in the main of many Industrial Schools, but they are, of course, not matters of deliberate intent and so the light in which they have been put by Mr. Dubois is false.

As may be seen from the File, Dr. McCabe has been pressing the Manager on these very matters for some years, and he has made efforts at improvement as far as his resources permit.

With regard to charge (3), viz that the sleeping quarters are ill-equipped and unheated, Mr. O Siochfhradha informs me that is a moot point among present day experts whether heating of sleeping quarters is desirable. He, for his part, however, is gradually prevailing on the authorities of the Girls' Schools to provide heating for the dormitories, but many Boys' Schools, including Artane, do not provide it. Mr. O Siochfhradha considers the sleeping equipment at Glin fairly good.

The Inspectors found no evidence of harshness or cruelty on the part of the staff or employees, and Mr. O Siochfhradha has stated to me that he is absolutely satisfied that it would not be in character for Br. Warrane or any other of the Brothers to treat the children unkindly.

Dr McCabe reports that the Manager has informed her that Mr. Dubois was dismissed from the post of night watchman in the school for insubordination.

The impression given to me by Mr. Dubois' letters and the Inspectors' Reports is

- *That Mr. Dubois grew to like the boys very much and to resent their being administered an occasional slap or cuff,*

- *That there may be some slight grounds for a charge of occasional severity, but that as regards clothing, food, etc. Mr. Dubois is probably unaware that the sole and entire income of the School was up to the present only 19s. capitation grant per week. Our inspectors are perfectly satisfied that the sum is stretched to its utter limit, and as far as they could see, the boys are happy and cheerful.*

- *That Mr. Dubois is a confirmed letter writer, as is evidenced by the number of letters that he has written to the boys in the School and by the fact that his turn of English is unusual in a night watchman. Incidentally, such phrases as "in the poor children they see Christ himself" seem, to me at least, too glib for their not particularly charitable context.*

I would guess that Mr. Dubois is a well-meaning person of rather unreserved character, and would advise taking no further notice of any missives he may forward. The Inspectors, however, intend to visit the school for some time more frequently than is customary, and it would seem well to do this.

Senior civil servants drafted and approved a letter to be sent by the Minister in reply to his colleague, who had moved in the meantime from the Department of Justice to the Department of Defence. Consideration was given as to whether it was more appropriate for the Minister to write directly to his colleague or for the respective private secretaries to communicate. It is not clear which course was adopted. The draft as prepared said:

> *That the Minister has had searching inquiries made and can find no convincing evidence to support the accusations made by Mr. Dubois.*

> *The fact that the financial resources of our industrial schools are in general rather limited makes it impossible for the authorities to supply other than plain food and clothing or to install equipment of the most up to date quality.*

> *With regard to the charge of harshness, unkindness and ill treatment of the boys, the Minister is assured that it would not be in character for the Brothers to permit such to occur, much less to be guilty of it themselves.*

> *It has been arranged, however, to inspect the school more frequently for some time to come.*

The Christian Brothers' submissions on this matter comment that the length of the investigation (approximately eight months) and "the number and seniority of the officers involved indicates that complaints were taken seriously by the State and that final decisions were not made lightly." They contend that the first letter sent by Mr. Dubois "set in motion a typical investigation by the Department involving unannounced visits by Dr. McCabe and the local school inspector." The letter to the Minister for Justice, they maintain, "lent urgency to the investigation," which eventually involved the secretary of the Department, the Minister's secretary and the Minister for Education.

The Department did not interview Mr. Dubois as part of their investigation. They did not investigate further whether Mr. Dubois retired due to health reasons, as stated by him, or was dismissed for insubordination, as asserted by the Manager. It does not appear that they conducted any spot check, as suggested by Mr. Dubois. The Department acknowledged internally that Mr. Dubois's criticisms of the clothing, food, and sleeping accommodation were "true in the main of many industrial schools." Mr. Dubois's concerns regarding the inexperienced chef and the often absent nurse could quite easily have been addressed and rectified. Neither were enquiries made about Mr. Dubois's predecessor who, it was alleged, regularly wielded a heavy leather strap and terrified the boys.

The Department wrote off Mr. Dubois's complaints as the outpourings of a man with a personal grievance. As a result, no thorough investigation was carried out.

A proper investigation of the complaints required that Mr. Dubois should have been interviewed. Such an interview was needed, not least because the Resident Manager had suggested a malicious motive for writing the letter and Dr. McCabe should have established whether this was the case.

Even when the Department did make findings, it did not explain where the facts came from. For example, there was no information as to how the Department concluded that "there may be some slight grounds for a charge of occasional severity" and, similarly, what investigations led them to the conclusion that the boys were administered "an occasional slap or cuff."

The Department acknowledged internally that three of the four charges he made were "true in the main of many industrial schools" and, by implication, they were true in respect of Glin. In other words, the boys were poorly clothed, and had no winter underwear, the food was meager, poor, and badly cooked, and the sleeping quarters were ill-equipped and unheated. They seemed to believe nothing needed to be done simply because such conditions were not peculiar to Glin but were quite widespread in such schools.

Despite the cursory nature of their inquiries, the Department was nevertheless prepared to inform another Minister in the Government that the minister for Education "has had searching inquiries made" and that there was "no convincing evidence to support the accusations made by Mr. Dubois."

Brother Jules

Brother Jules taught in a number of industrial schools; Carriglea, Artane, Tralee, and Glin, where he held the post of Superior for five years during the 1950s.

At an early stage, Br. Jules developed a reputation for being tough on his pupils. In the early 1930s, he came to the attention of the Provincial Council because of his harsh treatment of a pupil in Tralee who had a physical disability. This incident has been dealt with in the Tralee chapter. He was initially rejected from taking his perpetual vows. He was, however, allowed to take his vows the following year by a vote of three to one, notwithstanding a report describing him as:

> *Too exacting in school: little devotedness to study: "troublesome, cross grained," has not had a good record – doubtful candidate.*

The Superior General, Br. Noonan, wrote to Br. Jules congratulating him on taking his perpetual vows. In the course of the letter he stated:

> *You incline to the harsh side in school both in language and in inflicting bodily pain. Pupils hate sarcasm and they have a keen sense of what is just and fair in punishment. If you would secure respect for yourself and for your teaching be kind and just towards your pupils. It is said you are a poor student yourself. Perhaps it is due to your failure to make preparation for your work as a teacher that your pupils are made to suffer doubly.*

During Br. Jules's tenure as a Superior of Glin in the 1950s, the visiting brothers consistently complimented him on his management and dedication to the boys, and brothers who were interviewed by Br. McCormack for his report confirmed that a kinder regime was introduced following his appointment.

In his questionnaire for the congregation, completed in 1999, Br. Jules stated that, "There were no written rules regarding discipline. There was simply a general understanding of rules passed on from year to year." Despite holding the positions of Superior, School Manager, and Disciplinarian, he conceded that he had never seen the Rules and Regulations for Industrial Schools. He had no recollection of pupils being severely beaten. He dealt with absconders by making them feel ashamed of what they had done. He did not punish them.

He explained how he introduced new boys to the school:

> *When a new pupil came he would often be very upset. We had to point out to him that he was not wanted at home and convince him that life had not been that good at home; that we had taken him in, that he would be better off here.*

Br. Coyan, in an interview with Br. McCormack, recalled that Br. Jules did punish absconders by giving them a "baldy haircut and the kids didn't give a damn or they might be deprived of some privilege or other for a week or so."

Brother Marceau

Brother Marceau already had a bad record of violence towards boys when he was assigned to Glin in the early 1960s. He worked there for almost two years, between periods of service in Tralee Industrial School. Investigations have revealed a paper trail of documented cases of physical abuse by Br. Marceau in day and residential schools in which he taught. Accounts of Br. Marceau's conduct in the other institutions is dealt with in the Tralee chapter.

Prior to his time in Glin, Br. Marceau worked in Tralee and, before that, in a day school in Clonmel. During his four and a half years in Clonmel, there were four serious allegations of physical abuse against him. Three of the incidents resulted in the parents of the children complaining to the Superior, and the fourth incident was witnessed by another brother, who was so concerned over what he had seen that he warned the Superior to keep a close eye on Br. Marceau. When confronted in respect of complaints, Br. Marceau either minimized the seriousness of the incidents or emphatically denied that they had happened. He was issued with a Canonical Warning in the early 1960s. When the Superior of the Community received the fourth complaint from a parent later that year, he wrote that he was simply not prepared to deal with any more irate parents complaining about the ill-treatment of their children at the hands of Br. Marceau. He regarded Br. Marceau as a danger to the boys and simply unfit to be in charge of them. He begged for Br. Marceau to be removed from his school. Br. Marceau was transferred to St Joseph's Industrial School, Tralee.

The first Visitation Report following his transfer to Tralee recorded that this brother did not seem to be "quite normal and would appear to be deteriorating mentally." He was "lacking a good sense." The follow-up letter to the Resident Manager noted that he "may perhaps be inclined to be rather too exacting" and, accordingly, the Manager would have to ensure that his "zeal" for the children's progress did not get the better of him.

Br. Marceau was transferred to Glin later that year, where he remained for approximately two years, after which he was sent back to Tralee.

In the year following Br. Marceau's arrival in Glin, the Visitor remarked that Br. Marceau was still upset over the Canonical Warning he had received. Br. Marceau was convinced that there was a vendetta against him and had tried to have the Canonical Warning rescinded, but to no avail. The Visitor noted that, in Br. Marceau's view, the warning was "too severe a penalty for faults that were grossly exaggerated by a Superior who was prejudiced against him and in fact was out to get him, as he put it." He was bolstered in his opinion, having sought the advice of three priests on the matter, who unanimously agreed that the punishment did not fit the crime. The Visitor urged him to accept the situation and concentrate on his work in the school. He surmised that Br. Marceau was "not a vindictive type of man" and noted that he was very well regarded in the community.

It was not long before Br. Marceau once again came to the attention of the Provincial Council. Almost two years later, the Resident Manager wrote to the Provincial, notifying him of an incident that had recently taken place. Br. Marceau learned that a pupil had referred to him as "madman." He took the pupil to the Superior and the boy admitted the offence. The Superior slapped him on the palm of the hand in punishment.

Later that day, the boy reported to the infirmary with a pain in his jaw. His face was noticeably swollen and, when questioned by the Brother in charge of the infirmary, the boy reluctantly admitted that Br. Marceau had struck him on the face before he had brought him before the Superior. Br. Marceau denied the allegation. A week later, the swelling had not subsided and the local doctor examined the boy on his weekly visit. He recommended an x-ray as a precautionary measure, and it was discovered that the boy had a fractured jaw. He was detained in hospital for observation.

The Provincial wrote to Br. Marceau and requested an account of the incident. He responded the following day with a detailed version of events. He stated that he was aware that he was referred to by the nickname "madman" by the boys, because he was considered over-vigilant in his supervision of the dormitories, playgrounds, and toilets. On the day in question, he was made aware of the fact that a boy had referred to him by this name. He informed the boy's teacher of the matter and the two brothers questioned the boy. The boy admitted the allegation and, after being interrogated by Br. Marceau, he reluctantly disclosed the names of two other culprits. Br. Marceau accompanied him to the Superior's office and back to the classroom where he stated that the Superior "got him to apologise. Then I gave the boy a few slaps on the hands, but at no time during the incident did I beat him anywhere else."

The Provincial replied, admonishing Br. Marceau on his handling of the whole affair and, in particular, the manner in which he disregarded the Superior's authority. He warned, "You understand, I hope, that you have made a very bad mistake and that you are fortunate the consequences have not been more serious. (I am praying they will not be.)" He informed Br. Marceau that he would be transferred immediately to Tralee.

There is no mention in the letter from the Provincial that Br. Marceau had a history of serious physical assaults on pupils in other schools, including Tralee, the school to which he was being sent for the second time. Three days after Br. Marceau's untimely departure from Glin, a member of the Provincial Council conducted the annual Visitation of Glin. There was only a veiled reference to the incident that had resulted in Br. Marceau's transfer. The Visitor noted that Br. Marceau and another brother had encouraged tale-telling amongst the younger children and this had resulted in "the recent incident."

However, that was not the end of the matter. The Christian Brothers were obliged to notify the Department of Education of the fact that a boy had been hospitalized. A routine enquiry issued, requesting information on the manner in which the injury was sustained. The reply stated, "facial injury accidentally caused in the administration of punishment." The Resident Manager feared that the enquiry was the result of a Dáil question, and he asked a member of the Provincial Council to meet with a Department official. Br. Moynihan met Mr. MacUaid of the Department to discuss "the affair in Glin," and Mr. MacUaid made a note that Brother Moynihan was not sure whether the injury was the result of a blow from the strap or from collision during punishment, as the Consultor, who he had sent down to investigate the matter, "was vague on this point." He declined to divulge the name of the brother, only revealing that he had been transferred elsewhere. Mr. MacUaid noted that:

> *The Resident Manager of Glin is a kindly man and I under-stand that there is a good atmosphere in the school. Yet, there is the possibility that the coincidence of the official query and the Bundoran inquiry may have flushed a bird which other-wise might have lain concealed.*

The Department was somehow informed of the identity of the perpetrator, as the next letter was from Br. Marceau to the Department, in which he referred to a recent interview in Tralee with a Department official. He was outraged that such an allegation could have been made and stated:

> *I emphatically deny that I struck this boy on the face for a very insulting remark he made about me.*
>
> *I fail to understand how this false charge has been made against me. Therefore I have nothing to add to our recent conversation in St. Joseph Tralee...*

Despite the gaps in the documents it is clear that:

- The Department was aware that a boy in Glin was injured so severely that his jaw was fractured and he was hospitalized.
- Br. Marceau was the most likely perpetrator of the injury, despite his denial.
- As a result of the incident, the Provincial Council saw fit to have him transferred from the school to another residential school.

- Br. Marceau's violence was documented in congregation records.
- The congregation was in dereliction of its duty of care by sending Br. Marceau to Glin, and then transferring him back to Tralee, despite his violent treatment of boys.
- The Department was also in dereliction of duty, as it did not voice any concerns regarding the incident and was content to let the matter lie.

The Congregation asked surviving brothers who had worked in residential institutions to complete questionnaires in relation to their views of life in industrial schools. Br. Marceau completed one such questionnaire in 1999. In it, he stated that it was more difficult to mould industrial schoolboys because they lacked character. There was no written code of discipline; there was instead a code of practice, which was passed from one brother to another. His mentor had advised him not to become too friendly with the boys. Each brother was expected to handle his own discipline problems. He stated that he was humane in his treatment of the boys, but accepted that he also used the "hamh laidir." In addition, he used competition between the boys and a rewards system to maintain control.

In his view, most of the allegations of abuse made against brothers were false. He thought that there were too many brothers accused for the matter to make sense. He denied all allegations of abuse made against him.

- Glin had a severe, systemic regime of corporal punishment.
- Brothers with a known propensity for physically abusive behavior were sent to Glin.

SEXUAL ABUSE

Brother Buiron

Brother Buiron spent almost seven years in Glin in the early 1940s. Prior to this, while resident in Artane, he confessed to the Superior that he had sexually abused a boy in the infirmary, where he was working. It appears from minutes of a General Council Meeting held at that time that there were a number of incidents. Br. Buiron was called before the Superior General and admitted the offences. The Superior General wrote to the Provincial:

> *I sent for Br. B today and told him of the risk we ran in retaining him in the congregation and gave him until tomorrow morning at ten o'clock to consider if he would apply for a dispensation or stand trial. I will let you know the result. He is a great danger to us. Two brothers were hanged in Canada within the past two years for murder of their victims after such offence. A brother of a community in charge of an industrial school in Rome awaits his trial for the murder of a boy in the school who told of his offence to his Superior. The school is closed and the community disbanded.*

Br. Buiron refused to apply for a dispensation and appeared before the General Council. A vote was taken, but instead of sending him for trial as predicted by the Superior General, it was unanimously agreed that Br. Buiron should be retained in the congregation. He was given "...the first canonical warning, threatened with expulsion, and given a penance; the daily recital of the Miserere." The Superior General wrote to the Provincial informing him of the outcome of the vote, which was taken "after very mature deliberation." He continued:

I told him that you would send him the official warning when writing to him and giving him his location (which will be very difficult I fear). He shows signs of the greatest repentance. He told us he was not sure (of the boys' name) and that he told him after the first offence that he (Br. B) would now have to leave the brothers.

Br. Buiron was immediately moved to Cork, where he remained until he was transferred to Glin.

Brother Piperei

Brother Piperei taught in Glin for six years during the 1940s. He had previously served in Letterfrack and Tralee. Following his time in Glin, he was transferred to Salthill. In Letterfrack, he was the subject of a serious complaint that he was sexually interfering with boys. A full account of the case is contained in the chapter on Letterfrack. An allegation against him was investigated, but only to the extent that he was asked about it by a Visitor, and subsequently gave lengthy written account by way of letter. The explanation offered by the brother ought to have given rise to increased unease rather than to have allayed suspicion. He later taught in Cork, where his conduct in relation to young girls caused him to be removed urgently and relocated in retirement in the Midlands.

These Bothers were sent to Glin after complaints or suspicions of sexual abuse in other industrial schools. Given the risk of such behavior being repeated, it was reckless to transfer them to a residential school, where the children were particularly vulnerable as they had no recourse to their families.

JOHN E. MORRISON

NEGLECT AND EMOTIONAL ABUSE

Visitation Reports and Department of Education Inspection Reports

In 1938, the visitor commented on the boys' appearance:

> *Nobody can fail to remark the contrast between an Industrial School boy in his everyday rig and the appearance of even the poorest boys attending our Day Schools. The Industrial School boy seems to have no appreciation of personal cleanliness and tidiness of dress.*

The following year, the Visitor recorded that the school had received a favourable report from the Department Inspector, but he found the top class weak in arithmetic, handwriting, and letter writing. In addition, the brother in charge of this class had unilaterally decided to abandon the teaching of Irish. The Visitor remarked that he "ought show more zeal for their welfare." He noted that one of the other two teaching brothers was also a poor teacher. The Visitor was critical of the boys' clothing, some of which was simply unfit for use and should be discarded. He complained about the heavy boots the boys wore, which were badly repaired, making them "unsightly, unwieldy things." He was pleased to see that the boys now had good shoes for Sunday.

In June 1940, the Visitor said that the yard was surfaced in coarse gravel, which made it unsuitable as a play area. He found only one of the teachers, out of a complement of five, satisfactory. He observed, "the teaching staff here, as in the other industrial schools I visited this year, as weak. The type of boy in the industrial schools needs to have devoted, zealous, and self-sacrificing teachers."

The treacherous condition of the schoolyard continued to receive mention in the Visitation Reports and Department Inspection Reports, but it was not until 1955 that the necessary work was undertaken.

The 1941 Visitation Report listed repairs and improvements that were necessary, including the faulty hot water and heating system, and that the play hall was "cold, unsightly and dilapidated" and needed to be replaced. The teachers, once again, came in for criticism, with only one of them regarded as satisfactory. Br. Young was not impressed by the standard of work in the two trades being taught, namely boot-making and tailoring. The workshops were unsuitable and, in instances, dangerous.

In 1942, the Visitor approved of the new spacious play hall, which had been built for the boys. Water pipes continued to present problems, resulting in an insufficiency of water to the boys' lavatories. The teacher in charge of the two junior classes had fifty-nine pupils in his class, which made it very difficult to teach effectively.

Two years later, the Visitor found that "the literary side of the boys' education is somewhat over emphasized to the neglect of practical work." He drew attention to the fact that the only trades taught were tailoring and shoemaking. He noted that the boys' sanitary facilities were "entirely inadequate" and he was also critical of the laundry, which required renovations

The boys' lavatories came in for criticism once again during the Visitation in 1945. The Visitor noted that the "Boys' lavatories and bathroom are very primitive; there are no cisterns in the lavatories and boys have to carry water three times a day to flush them; I found a bad smell from them, they had not been flushed in the morning I saw them; it was about 11am. It would be advisable to attend to both lavatories and bathroom in the near future."

Of the overall population of 214 boys, there were 190 on the school register. The remaining twenty-four boys were employed for more than six hours each day on the farm or in the workshops. This group received thirty minutes of instruction in religious doctrine daily. He advised:

> *It is desirable that an hour a day extra should be afforded these boys to continue their education, especially as some of them had very little at the age of 14 years when they left*

off school work. Subjects such as English, Private Reading,
Arithmetic, etc. should interest and be useful to such boys.

In May 1946, the Visitor observed that the premises were badly
laid out for the purposes of an industrial school, and that many
repairs and alterations were necessary. The boys' bathroom came
in for particular criticism, as it was too small and badly fitted. The
yards and approaches to the Institution were in very bad condition
and posed a hazard. Some of the wire mattresses required overhaul-
ing, although he appreciated the difficulty in obtaining wire. He
predicted that a sizable sum of money would have to be expended
on the school before long. The recurring theme of the inadequacy
of trades training and education was once again aired. He observed:

> *It is very difficult to place boys in the trades when they have*
> *to go out and many who have been trained to shoemaking*
> *or tailoring have to go to farm work. These are much handi-*
> *capped and are not a success. The trades or farm boys do not*
> *receive any education when once they begin their respective*
> *trades. This is unfortunate, as they soon forget much of what*
> *they have learnt.*

He noted complaints that the school was understaffed, and recommended that a brother who could undertake some school work
would be useful.

In December 1946, Dr. McCabe visited the School and recorded
that the premises were clean and in good condition and that the
children were well cared for and happy. However, she noted a major
deficiency, which was subsequently set out in a follow-up letter from
the Department to the Superior in December:

> *It is reported, however, that a number of the boys have not*
> *gained in weight and that a few have actually lost 2 or 3*
> *lbs during the year. These boys who do not put on weight*

normally should be specially watched and they should be given such additional or special food as the School Medical Officer may prescribe.

- *Porridge should be served at breakfast. Each boy should be allowed at least a quarter of a pound of meat at each meal at which meat is served.*

- *The boy's everyday clothing should be improved.*

- *The sanitary annexe should be kept in better order.*

- *Rubber aprons and Wellington boots should be provided for the boys in the laundry.*

- *There is need for the provision of a new bathing annexe.*

- *The dampness in the walls of the dormitories should be attended to. It is understood that you will arrange to have this matter attended to during the summer of 1947.*

Additional points in her original report were that the dormitory walls had not been re-plastered as promised and remained damp, and there also remained room for improvement in the boys' clothing. She noted that the outdoor sanitation annexe was better kept than previously. Overall, she noted a general improvement in all departments.

In May 1948, the Visitor noted that the damp walls in the boys' dormitories remained untreated, as did the play yard:

The surface of the playground is completely gone and the rough stone foundation revealed and in dirty weather the surface must be something approaching a morass and as in this establishment, owing to the fact that the various sections are completely cut off from one another and that the boys have to go out into the open air when passing from one to the

*other, this mud is carried on their boots into all departments
and particularly the chapel.*

He drew attention to a pattern he had noticed from visiting other institutions, which was the lack of facilities for the boys' recreation:

*During the recreations there seems to be a universal tendency
to just turn the boys loose in the playing field or to herd them
into an empty hall and then to let them fend for themselves.
A lot of them seemed to just loll around. Obviously such boys
should be kept well occupied in an interesting manner. There
seems to be a very great need for a much more generous supply
of apparatus for games both outdoor and indoor. Very little
seems to be done in the matter of supplying suitable reading
material for them. Physical training is only carried out in a
rather haphazard manner if at all.*

Although the deteriorating condition of the premises was noted in various reports, the congregation was reluctant to invest in repairs and renovations when the viability of the school was very much in question.

Dr. McCabe remarked, in Medical Inspection Reports completed during the 1950s, that she was satisfied with improvements to the boys' diet. During an inspection in February 1954, she noted many improvements in the school. A new boiler had been installed, the dormitories painted, a carpenter's shop added, new equipment introduced to the kitchen, and new blankets and bedspreads acquired for the beds.

The Visitation Report in May 1954 was not quite so positive. The report noted that the boys' play hall was small and "somewhat depressing," but the Superior asserted that the boys had plenty to amuse themselves with during the frequent rainy periods. The Visitor found the shower facilities rather primitive, although the Superior assured him that improvements had been made. He was glad to see that the boys had new boots and sandals "so that there was none of the heavy clattering of boots that is such an undesirable feature of some of our industrial schools."

The Visitor in 1958 expressed concern at the standard of trades training in Glin. Tailoring and shoe mending were still the only trades, but in the previous five years only one boy had directly benefited from the training he'd received. Upon leaving Glin, practically all of the boys went to work on farms, and many did not have an aptitude for it. The Visitor was satisfied with the boys' diet and clothing, although he was critical of their footwear.

The Visitor made similar findings as regards trades training in his report the following year. He recorded that, despite the existence of a carpentry shop, carpentry was not taught. He believed that machines rather than people were used in the trades in which the boys were instructed and jobs could not be secured for them. Boys tended to work on farms before drifting off to England or into the army. He supported the Superior's suggestion that a brother who could teach arts and crafts be drafted onto the staff in order to "take some of the dullness out of their lives." He added, "the evening is long here and occupation for the boys is necessary."

In 1959 the Visitor expressed concern at the state of disrepair of the school during his visitation, although he noted that "repairs are out of the question owing to falling numbers and meager government grants." However, he advised that the fire escape, which was in a dangerous condition, be attended to as it presented a danger and "could scarcely be used in an emergency." He queried the unusually high level of failure at the Primary Certificate examinations, and noted that the children were weak at arithmetic.

The Visitor in 1961 made the customary remarks about the state of disrepair of the premises. He also commented that, when the boys left Glin, they often seemed very lost in the world:

Some of them do not easily fit into their new surroundings especially those who have never known what family life should be. Many drift from job to job and eventually emigrate. The general impression of the visitor would be, I think, that the institution fulfills a useful purpose and many pupils who have been the victims of circumstances and brought up under sordid conditions are given a fresh start and are well prepared for life.

The Visitor in 1964 stated:

The boys' toilets are bad and require to be completely renovated. Being in the open and uncovered they are exposed and in wintertime this is severe on the boys. They would require to be replaced by new toilets but owing to the uncertainty with regard to the future of industrial schools this is scarcely to be recommended. The boys' kitchen is in the same bad condition as it has always been.

The following year, the Visitor acknowledged that a substantial sum had been spent on updating the boys' kitchen, but additional renovations had been put on hold pending a decision on the future of the school. The school closed in 1966.

HOME LEAVE

Home leave was first granted in 1924 and was for a maximum of seven days per annum. It was extended in 1935 to fourteen days, following an unofficial suggestion by the Cussen Commission prior to its final report. Following publication of the report, the period was once again extended to twenty-one days per year, and the discretion regarding who went on home leave was transferred to the Resident

Manager, who was thus allowed a certain degree of latitude in determining the length of a child's leave.

In 1948, a further ten days were allocated, thus increasing the total to thirty-one days.

Some figures for home leave from Glin between 1942 and 1966 were compiled by Br. McCormack in his report. These are available primarily from the Christian Brother Annals and are set out below:

1942: In July about 80 of the boys spent three weeks with their parents or friends (Annals).

1944: 75 boys went on home leave (Annals).

1945: 110 boys went home for a three-weeks holiday in July (Annals).

1953: In August all but three of the boys returned from holidays in their homes. One of these had been taken to England by his mother, but after negotiation he was returned to the school (Annals).

1955: About 50 boys went home on holidays (Annals).

1958: About 50 boys went home on holidays (Annals).

1961: About 40 of the boys got a fortnight's holiday with families who offered to take them (VR 19.4)

1962: In July, 36 boys went home for a month holidays (Annals).

1965: In July some boys went home for their holidays. In August, 36 boys went to Carne, Co. Wexford for 3 weeks holiday. Transport was provided by the Limerick Lions Club (Annals).

1966: In July, 20 boys went home on holiday and 30 went to Knockadoon. All returned on 1 August (Annals).

These figures are not absolute and are provided without context, and are even contradicted on occasion by Department of Education figures; for example, in 1942, 70 not 80 boys went on home leave and , in 1944, 74 boys went on leave out of a total of 207. Some years are also missing, but can be found in records provided by the Department of Education; for instance, in 1948, the Department recorded that just 28 boys returned home that summer.

The Department's desire to extend home leave to a wider number of children, for a greater period of time, met with resistance from a number of Resident Managers, Glin included. On 22nd November 1944, the Manager of Glin wrote to the Industrial Schools Branch of the Department of Education, defending the decision to send only seventy-four children out of a total of 207 on home leave. The Manager stated, "I kept them in the school because I had no guarantee that their friends would be able to maintain and take care of them." He also stated in this letter that every boy in the school wrote to relatives regarding the home leave, with seventy-four positive replies, six negative replies, and no replies in the remaining cases. Closing the letter, he remarked, "I did not consider it advisable to send boys on holidays to parents and relatives who did not reply."

This hostility to home leave emerged most strongly when, in 1949, the Department of Education proposed to extend the maximum period to six weeks in a calendar year. Just seven schools were in favour of the proposal and thirty-seven were against it, including Glin. The Resident Managers, in a letter dated 7th June 1949, stated their reasons in very clear terms:

> *It was pointed out that when the children return from Home Leave there is always a marked dis-improvement in manners and conduct; they are often very discontented, impatient of control, and physically and morally upset., All this is highly detrimental to the general spirit of the School, and it takes children quite a long time to settle down again to the ordinary routine.*

> *Numbers of them return ill-fed and sickly, in an unkempt condition, with clothes in a filthy condition. It takes weeks to get rid of the vermin. Sometimes their language is vile, having picked it up in undesirable quarters. And for some such considerations some Managers suggested that instead of extending the Home Leave period, it should be shortened.*

Industrial School children generally belong to the poorest families and the home conditions are often most unsuitable and undesirable. It was mentioned where a family of eight lived and slept in one room; also where a father, two girls and a boy slept in the one bed, while the mother, dying of T. B. was in a corner in a bed supplied by the Corporation.

A high percentage of these children are illegitimate and their mothers are not just what they should be; others have been the victims of circumstances getting into trouble because parents or guardians failed to exercise proper control. And as it was by order of the Court that these children were committed to the Schools, it stands to reason it would not be for their betterment to allow them to return to such undesirable conditions for protracted periods.

It was also said that children who could with safety be allowed six weeks' Home Leave should not be in any Industrial School; they should be discharged to their homes and not be allowed to be parasites living on public moneys.

While many of these points may have been true, the tone of the letter shows very little understanding of the need for family contact, In Submissions, the Christian Brothers commented:

The general unsuitability of the children's homes on account of poverty, overcrowding, and lack of parental control also figured among the reasons for opposing the proposal and some Managers (number not given) even suggested that shortening of Home Leave would be a better option.

They added that there was "genuine concern for the children in the opposition to extending home leave."

AFTERCARE

Seven hundred and sixty-one boys passed through the school between 1940 and 1966. Forty percent (308) of these boys were discharged to members of their family. According to the Dunleavy Report, the School Register showed that the boys were discharged to the following relatives:

	1940-1947	1947-1966	Total
Discharged to father	50	79	129
Discharged to mother	35	60	95
Discharged to parents	20	7	27
Discharged to aunt	7	11	18
Discharged to grandmother	5	5	10
Discharged to uncle	4	10	14
Discharged to sister	4		4
Discharged to grandfather	4		4
Discharged to brother	2	5	7
SUBTOTAL	131	177	308

As can be seen, 81% of those discharged to a relative went to a parent or parents.

According to the Dunleavy Report, aftercare beyond one year was provided to boys as follows:

Years	Boys receiving more than one	%
1940 – 1947	68	18%
1947 – 1966	61	15%

It is likely that most of these boys were discharged to places of employment , and had no relatives to look after them. The brother in charge of aftercare made notes on pay, living conditions, and contentedness of the boy.

Records were kept of the kinds of employment found for the boys. The following table taken from the Dunleavy Report covers the period:

Employment	1940-1947	1947-1966	Total
Farm boy	87	76	163
House boy	21	43	64
Hotel worker	10	16	26
Boot maker*	7	3	10
Shop boy	5	1	6
Tailor*	4	1	5
Religious order*		3	3
Cook*		2	2
Builders labourer	1	1	2
Blacksmith	1		1

Monumental sculptor*		1	1
Subtotal	136	147	283

*Skilled or semi-
skilled work

Eighty-nine percent of the boys went into unskilled work on farms, or as houseboys or hotel workers. Sixteen boys between 1947 and 1966 went on to join the army. A further fourteen were charged with criminal offences.

The congregation in its Submissions, made the point that trade unions had made it difficult for boys to enter trades. However, a number of Visitation Reports pointed out that the limited trades taught were effectively useless to the boys upon leaving the Institution, as they were dictated by the requirements of the school rather than the kind of training that would prepare the boys for work.

SUBMISSIONS OF THE CHRISTIAN BROTHERS

The Submissions made by the congregation on issues of neglect of the boys in Glin drew attention first to the General Inspection Reports of the Department of Education, which it stated were generally very favourable. It said that the process of inspection as carried out by Dr. Anna McCabe was thorough and had good follow-up. At the end of each inspection as carried out by Dr. Anna McCabe, Dr. McCabe made recommendations orally to the Manager of the School, which were then followed up by a letter from the Department, formally listing the recommendations. The process came to a close with a letter of confirmation from the Manager that the required altera-tions and improvements had been made. The congregation contend that the Resident Manager responded promptly to the reports. The reality, however, is that the Department Inspections were a good deal less effective than the congregation's description would suggest.

The congregation also drew attention to favourable entries in the Visitation Reports. They included the statement in 1946 that the boys were well clothed and fed, and in 1949 and 1950 there were favourable comments about the variety and quantity of food.

The Submissions pointed out that Inspection Reports recorded improvements in recreational and cultural facilities, as well as holiday arrangements, from the end of the 1940s. Visitation Reports and Community Annals also reported the provision of a variety of facilities. As against that, the reports, which were quoted at paras 1.147 and 1.149 above, drew attention to the lack of recreation for the boys in Glin and that life was tedious for them.

The brothers cited documentary records, indicating the availability of cultural and sporting activities. These included a choir, dancing classes, an orchestra, drama, and boxing.

In respect of education, it was pointed out that, from 1952 onwards, small numbers of boys in each year attended outside secondary schools or vocational schools.

The Congregation conceded in regard to vocational training:

> *As regards the standards reached in the shops, it is doubtful if it went much beyond repairs and mending... However, judging by the very poor record of placement of boys in boot-making and tailoring, the skills most of the boys had to offer were not very considerable.*

The congregation contended that the Medical Inspection Reports were also favourable, that the medical records were well kept, and that the local doctor visited the school regularly. On the subject of dental treatment, they suggested that the number of boys referred for treatment was quite low. Quoting the Medical Reports, therefore, the general picture was one of compliance with the standards set out by Dr. McCabe, who was satisfied when the school met with her requirements and was also very appreciative of Managers' efforts to improve conditions for the residents. Healthcare was satisfactory, as recorded in the documents that are available. Similarly, hygiene was satisfactory. There are, however, very critical entries in the reports, particularly the Visitation Reports as disclosed.

The Congregation Submission was selective when referring to the available documentation, making no reference, for example, to significant criticisms in its own Visitation Reports.

DIFFERENCES BETWEEN VISITATION REPORTS AND INSPECTION REPORTS

There was a marked contrast between the Christian Brothers' Visitation Reports and the Department of Education Inspection Reports. The former were more in-depth and thorough, whereas the latter tended to be more cursory. The Visitation Reports were consistently critical of the dilapidated state of the school, and concerns about the damp walls in the dormitories, the atrocious state of the lavatories, and the treacherous state of the schoolyard were expressed. Dr. McCabe also made reference to these issues but not with the same sense of urgency. She did not make any reference to the effect that such sub-standard facilities might have on the children.

In some Visitation Reports, when the brothers noted the shabby state of the boys' clothing, no corresponding comment was made by Dr. McCabe. When she did note that the boys' clothing was tattered and patched, she did not press the matter or make suggestions as to how shortages in supplies could be addressed.

The brothers conceded in the Visitation Report of 1948 that there was little in the way of stimulating recreational facilities for the boys, but this was not an issue raised by Dr. McCabe.

The standard of education was another area where there were conflicting reports. The Visitation Reports were very negative about the standard of education and trades training in the school. It was not an issue that came within Dr. McCabe's remit, but the Department's Education Inspector made a favourable report on the school and did not pick up on the criticisms of the Visitors.

The limited trades available were dictated by the requirements of the school, rather than the kind of training needed to prepare the boys for work. A number of Visitation Reports pointed out that these trades were effectively useless to the boys upon leaving the institution. Boys were ill-prepared for the outside world; they did not fare well after being discharged and often tended to drift from job to job before ending up in England or joining the army.

Dr. McCabe's Inspection Reports, particularly in later years, would suggest that the inspections were not particularly probing, and were, in many respects, superficial. In areas where she did make criticisms, she did not tend to suggest practical solutions to the problems.

A comparison of both the Department and Visitation Reports suggests that the Visitation Reports provided a more reliable source of information about conditions in the School.

GENERAL CONCLUSIONS

- Glin had a severe, systemic regime of corporal punishment.
- The congregation transferred two brothers to Glin, despite evidence or suspicion of sexually abusing boys in another institution under the control of the Christian Brothers. This decision protected both the congregation and the brothers but endangered the boys in Glin.
- Documentary sources revealed serious deficiencies in the physical care, facilities, accommodation, education, training, and aftercare in Glin Industrial School.

- Problems affecting the standard of care in Glin persisted, despite being reported by both the congregation's Visitor and the Department of Education Inspectors.
- Glin Industrial School failed in its fundamental requirement to provide care, education, and training for the boys.
- The Department of Education failed in its supervisory duties. Its role was protective of the institution and its response to serious complaints was cursory and dismissive.

In Ireland, the Industrial School Act of 1868 established industrial schools to care for "neglected, orphaned and abandoned children."

In England, the 1857 Industrial Schools Act was intended to solve problems of juvenile delinquency, by removing poor and neglected children from their home environment to a boarding school. The Act allowed magistrates to send disorderly children to a residential industrial school. An 1876 Act led to non-residential day schools of a similar kind.

There were similar arrangements in Scotland, where the Industrial Schools Act came into force in 1866. The schools cared for neglected children and taught them a trade, with an emphasis on preventing crime. Some of these schools were known as reformatories or, later, as approved schools.

IRISH INDUSTRIAL SCHOOLS

The following schools were run by religious orders and funded by the public:

- Our Lady of Succour, Newtownforbes
- St. Patrick's Industrial School, Kilkenny, Ireland
- St. Vincent's Industrial School, Goldenbridge, Dublin, Ireland
- St. Conleth's reformatory School, Daingean

- St. Joseph's Industrial School, Letterfrack
- St. Joseph's Industrial School, Kilkenny, Ireland
- St. Joseph's Industrial School, Whitehall, Dublin Ireland
- Artane Industrial School, Dublin, Ireland
- St. Michael's Industrial School for Girls, Wexford
- St. Michael's Industrial School for Junior boys, Cappoquin, Co. Waterford
- St. Vincent's (House of charity) Industrial School for Junior Boys, Drogheda, Co. Louth
- St. Vincent's Industrial School for Girls, Limerick
- St. Vincent's Industrial School, Goldenbridge, Inchicore, Dublin 8
- St. Ann's Industrial School for Girls and Junior Boys, Renmore, Lenaboy, Co. Galway
- St. Anne's Reformatory School for Girls, Kilmacud, Co. Dublin
- St. Augustine's Industrial School for Girls, Templemore, Co. Tipperary
- St. Bernard's Industrial School for Girls, Fethard, Dundrum, Co. Tipperary
- St. Bridgid's Industrial School for Girls, Loughrea, Co. Galway
- St. Coleman's Industrial School for Girls, Cobh/Rushbrook, Co. Cork
- St. Columba's Industrial School for Girls, Westport, Co. Mayo
- St. Conleth's Reformatory School for Boys, Daingean, Co. Offaly
- St. Dominick's Industrial School for Girls, Waterford
- St. Finbarr's Industrial School for Girls, Sundays Well, Mary mount, Cork
- St. Francis Xavier's Industrial School for Girls and Junior Boys, Ballaghadereen, Co. Roscommon
- St. Francis' Industrial School for Girls, Cashel, Co. Tipperary
- St. George's Industrial School for Girls, Limerick
- St. John's Industrial School for Girls, Birr, Co. Offaly

- St. Joseph's Industrial School for Boys, Passage West, Co. Cork
- St. Joseph's Industrial School for Boys, Tralee, Co. Kerry
- St. Joseph's Industrial School for Girls and Junior Boys, Ballinasloe, Co. Galway
- St. Joseph's Industrial School for Girls and Junior Boys, Clifden, Co. Galway
- St. Joseph's Industrial School for Girls and unior Boys, Liosomoine, Killarney, Co. Kerry
- St. Joseph's Industrial School for Girls, Cavan
- St. Joseph's Industrial School for Girls, Dundalk, Co. Louth
- St. Joseph's Industrial School for Girls, Kilkenny
- St. Joseph's Industrial School for Girls, Mallow, Co. Cork
- St. Joseph's Industrial School for Girls, Summerhill, Athlone, Co. Westmeath
- St. Joseph's Industrial School for Girls, Whitehall, Drumcondra, Dublin 9
- St. Joseph's Industrial School for Senior Boys, Glin, Co. Limerick
- St. Joseph's Industrial School for Senior Boys, Ferryhouse, Clonmel, Co. Tipperary
- St. Joseph's Industrial School for Senior Boys, Greenmount, Cork
- St. Joseph's Industrial School for Senior Boys, Salthill, Co. Galway
- St. Joseph's Industrial School for Girls, Limerick
- St. Kyran's Industrial School for Junior Boys, Rathdrum, Co. Wicklow
- St. Laurence's Industrial School for Girls, Sligo
- St. Laurence's Industrial School, Finglas, Dublin 11
- St. Martha's Industrial School for Girls, Bundoran, Co. Donegal
- St. Mary's Industrial School, Lakelands, Sandymount, Dublin 4

CPSIA information can be obtained
at www.ICGtesting.com
Printed in the USA
BVHW031415250321
603272BV00011B/520

9 781525 577000